FIVE ESSENTIAL INGREDIENTS
FOR BUSINESS SUCCESS

Five Essential Ingredients for Business Success

Stories and Lessons from Three
of the UK's Greatest Restaurants

CHRIS PARKER

First published in 2012 by

Ardra Press
PO Box 100
Cottingham
HU16 9AB
United Kingdom
www.ardrapress.co.uk

ISBN: 9780954867874

British Library Cataloguing in Publication Data
A CIP record for this book can be obtained from the British Library

Designed and typeset by Julie Martin

Printed and bound by TJ International Ltd, Padstow, Cornwall

Cover design by Ciaron Lee Marlow: www.rockers-going-starwars.co.uk

For Syd,
For starting it all by taking me into a restaurant
for the first time.

'You find what you search for.'

Epiah Khan

Contents

Acknowledgements

My sincere thanks to all of the staff at Gidleigh Park, Le Manoir aux Quat'Saisons and The Waterside Inn for their help and patience. Most especially, thank you to the following:

Gidleigh Park
Michael Caines, Damien Bastiat, Andrew Foulkes, Edouard Oger, Scott Andrews.

Le Manoir aux Quat'Saisons
Raymond Blanc, Philip Newman-Hall, Gary Jones, Benoît Blin, Mourad Ben Tefka, Julia Murrell, Anne Marie Owens.

The Waterside Inn
Michel Roux Snr, Alain Roux, Diego Masciaga, Frédéric Poulette.

Thanks also to my friends and colleagues at Nottingham Trent University for their much needed support and advice; to Ronan for his publishing bravery; and, of course, to 'M' for putting up with it all – and everything else.

Introduction

'Excellence is a better teacher than mediocrity.
The lessons of the ordinary are everywhere.
Truly profound and original insights are to be
found only in studying the exemplary.'

Warren G. Bennis

This is a book about three exemplary restaurants. They are:

1. Gidleigh Park (2 Michelin stars)
2. Le Manoir aux Quat'Saisons (2 Michelin stars)
3. The Waterside Inn (3 Michelin stars)

The research and subsequent writing of this book was based on
a two-fold premise:

1. A study of exemplary restaurants will provide lessons and
   reveal insights from which all organisations, irrespective of
   their purpose or industry, can learn.
2. Stories about these restaurants can be entertaining and
   inspirational as well as educational.

Why exemplary restaurants?
For the following reasons:

a) The very best restaurants are committed to producing both
   an excellent product and excellent customer service and,
   unlike most other businesses, in restaurants the kitchen
   team (product development) and the front of house team
   (customer service) have to work cooperatively, side by

side, in real time in order to achieve their clearly defined outcomes.

b) This requires not only excellent teamwork and the sharing of individual expertise, but also excellent communication between teams.

c) These standards of excellence have to be achieved and maintained whilst working within time-framed, highly pressured situations, which are under constant scrutiny and can be assessed and reported upon by professional bodies and/or customers at any time.

d) These standards of excellence have to be maintained without customers, or professional assessors, noticing any obvious effort.

e) The very best restaurants have a clear and consistent sense of their identity and the 'world' into which they invite their guests; they understand all aspects and levels of their product and the entirety of the customer experience.

f) All staff within these restaurants perform repetitive routines and tasks as if for the first time, every time.

g) These restaurants are very successful at selling high-end luxury products and experiences, even during times of recession.

h) They manage to create, and meet, very high customer expectations consistently.

And, wonderfully, the first premise was proven right. Each individual restaurant provided specific learning and insights relating to the above and, most interestingly, they all shared five overarching lessons that I will identify and discuss in Part 2 of the book.

So, can other organisations really learn from the stories and lessons provided here? Yes! Obviously those in the hospitality and catering industry will relate automatically to the learning offered. However, any organisation that needs to create and ensure great products and/or exceptional customer service, develop and maintain brilliant teamwork, outstanding internal and external communications, a clear sense of corporate identity, consistency of delivery and repeat custom, can benchmark against the examples described.

The first part of the book is written as a collection of stories because stories are mankind's oldest teaching mechanism. Stories engage and entertain us. They introduce and reveal individuals and the characters of both people and places. They provide information and yet they are far more emotive and, therefore, more memorable than just a collection of data. Stories also reflect the ultimate purpose of the restaurants themselves, which is to create positive memory-stories that their guests take away[1] with them.

Elizabeth Coatsworth, the American poet and children's author, wrote the line:

'But calm, white calm, was born into a swan.'

The three restaurants in this book seek to provide their customers with calm, effortless excellence, their aim being to create a multi-sensory experience that will live as a memory forever. Unlike the swan, though, their calm elegance is not the result of birth, but rather of a commitment to achieving the very highest standards. It reflects years of hard work, attention to detail and a continual search for improvement. It is why we can all learn from what they have to offer.

Apart from their shared purpose and commitment, the restaurants also reflect the very significant French influence on British gastronomy. The Waterside Inn was established by Michel Roux Snr, a man who, with his brother Albert, led a gastronomic revolution in Britain through both the quality of their cuisine and their commitment to providing educational opportunities. The Roux Scholarship, founded in 1985, has encouraged and helped produce generations of great chefs and continues to do so. Raymond Blanc, the owner of Le Manoir aux Quat'Saisons, has also played his role in developing both individual talent and

---

1 And that is the only reference to a take-away you will find in this book!

industry practice by training many chefs who have gone on to achieve Michelin stars. One of these, now acknowledged as a culinary superstar in his own right, is Michael Caines, the Executive Head Chef at Gidleigh Park. Michael also studied in France with the 3-Michelin-starred chefs Bernard Loiseau and Joel Robuchon.

Whilst our restaurants might all come from a common tradition and share a common purpose they are all unique, influenced as much by their location as they are by the creativity and personality of the chef and the individual and collective qualities of the staff. They each, to use a restaurant pun, have their own distinct flavour. They remind us that there are, indeed, different paths to the mountain top and that, no matter what route you take, the air inevitably gets thinner and the margins for error become less the higher you reach.

Ultimately, then, the teaching stories in this book are about the innate desire that some people have to be the very best in their chosen field, to pursue perfection, to reach ever-greater heights. They provide a behind-the-scenes insight into the people, cultures, strategies and systems of three outstanding businesses that are at the forefront of their industry. They reveal some of what it takes to achieve brilliance and they dare us to consider if we, too, really want to be brilliant.

And with that said, it is time to begin the first story...

PART ONE

The Stories

1

A Place in Time: Gidleigh Park, Devon

'We are creative only for a moment'
Michael Caines MBE

This is a story about the power of environments, both natural and man-made, and the impact they have on those who work in them and those who experience them as guests. It is a story about commitment, the willingness to adapt and the determination to succeed no matter what obstacles are encountered or what changes need to be made. At its heart this is a story about the joy and the challenges of the creative process.

The story of Gidleigh Park offers lessons about:
* The role environments play in creating influence
* Long-distance leadership
* Time management
* The need for adaptability
* The transience of creativity.

i) Finding Your Way
Gidleigh Park can be found in the heart of Dartmoor National Park, two miles east of the small Devonshire town of Chagford at the end of a winding single-track road. For those used to driving the high-hedged, sometimes tree-lined, often narrow cross-country Devonshire lanes, this is just one more occasion

when patience, caution and calmness come naturally to the fore. For those accustomed only to ample space and visibility when travelling, the last mile or so before reaching Gidleigh can make the sight of the elegant, beautifully understated house even more of a cause for celebration than it would otherwise be.

This final section of road twists and turns, instilling its own pace into travellers, demanding a gentle slowness, requiring them, quite literally, to look forwards as they gradually escape the hustle and bustle of whatever 'real' world they are temporarily leaving behind. It is easy to imagine those approaching Gidleigh for the first time asking themselves repeatedly, 'What will we see around the next bend?' only to discover that the answer to their question is, in fact, another bend. There are occasional houses, however, reminders that this road is a daily thoroughfare for some. What is unusual here is not the road, but rather what waits at the end of it. Of course, for the first-time visitor, the sense of 'so near and yet so far' is as inescapable as the route itself. Surely, sometime soon, any moment now, the destination will be reached? And then, just when the question might change to, 'Are you sure this is the right road?' a sign encourages all to 'Keep heart'; the house, it assures, is just half a mile away.

It is all the reassurance that is needed. It is also the first indication that those responsible for Gidleigh Park recognise the ways their location can influence visitors and that they seek to manage these influences at every turn. The sign provides both a welcome and an encouragement in a manner that reflects the storybook nature of what lies ahead. This is not a business ensconced within a building. This is a place that many might call a *destination restaurant*. Only it is far more than just an award-winning restaurant. And the destination is far more than this beautiful part of England's tourist landscape.

Gidleigh breathes life into her surroundings just as the wind creates movement in the trees that line the route. She has a presence that extends out into the local villages and towns and far beyond. Locals talk about her with respect, warmth and admiration, much as they might talk of a well-known celebrity who is at once an international figure and yet also a vital, if rarely encountered, part of their own community. Gidleigh's character is as real and, in some ways, as mysterious as the moor itself. And there is only one way to experience it fully. You have to follow the road.

Not long now. One final, gentle S-bend, an incline that is more noticeable on foot than in a car, an expanse of ground opening to your right and Gidleigh appears, looking down from her slightly elevated position across the gardens and fields to the hills at the opposite end of the valley. The North Teign river runs down from the woodland to your left and underneath the road, separating the more obviously manicured, terraced gardens from the rest. You might notice the path, parallel to the water, the tennis court further to your right, or the vegetable and herb garden just above that. You might notice how trees wrap themselves, discreetly distanced, around the house and grounds. You might notice any or all of these things, but in all probability your attention will be drawn instead to the house, to Gidleigh herself, described by Damien Bastiat, the Restaurant Manager, as 'the grand old lady in all her finery', timeless in her stillness and silence, waiting patiently to take you into her arms and complete the first part of your journey.

The Tudor-style house, with its dark wood and white exterior, shares an immediate sense of history and appropriateness, of belonging and craftsmanship. If the house seeks to make both staff and guests feel at home, so she, in turn, seems completely at home here, at the head of the valley, enveloped by the moor. If she were not this house, Gidleigh would be a classic, hand-made, ocean-going schooner, designed for purpose, beautiful to the eye, offering the promise of elegant transportation to another place. Only she is this house, this 'fine old lady', and she suggests a promise of her own, a promise first hinted at on the sign you passed just a moment or two ago.

It could have read, 'Gidleigh Park 800 metres' with an arrow pointing the way. It could have been as factual and emotionless as any other road sign. Only it wasn't. It asked you to 'Keep heart' because this place wants to touch the hearts of all those who visit. It is a place with a heart of its own, one that is serviced and kept well by the people who work here. Unlike the humans who experience her, though, Gidleigh has a life cycle stretching over several centuries, benefiting from repeated regeneration, the reflection of the need shared by many to maintain her through the ages.

The entrance to the house is lined with wellingtons, available for guests who have forgotten their own and yet want to follow one of Gidleigh's planned walks on the moor. On the walls are maps of the area, and four dated pictures of the house hang together in a simple frame. They date back to the sixteenth century. They provide illustrations, snapshots, from other times. They reinforce and explain the sense of belonging that pervades Gidleigh. You don't need to notice the pictures to realise, to *feel*, that Gidleigh is an integral and essential part of this setting.

Above the inner door is a carving that reads 'Once upon a time…' It is more than just a reminder of Gidleigh's history. It is another indication that this is a storybook place. 'Once upon a time…' is an invitation to take part in a journey, to travel in the storyteller's imagination to somewhere far removed from our usual experience. And yet here it is, waiting to greet guests upon their arrival. At first glance this invitation appears to be at their journey's end rather than at the beginning. At second glance, though, the message becomes clear: you have followed the road as far as you could, you have found your way here, and now the real journey begins…

It is a journey that is primarily inward in nature. Into the house first of all, into a place that is quintessentially English and that provides a sense of tranquillity, a peacefulness, that transcends culture or words, that simply *is*. Here the hustle and bustle of the guests' daily routines is left a long way behind. Here, surrounded by nature, cosseted by the comfort, the deliberately created homeliness of the house, time slows and guests can relax, travelling inwards into their own personal thoughts, their motivations for being here, recharging their batteries, feeding their senses and putting things in perspective. This is at the heart of the promise and purpose of Gidleigh Park. It is a promise given life by the creative people who work here.

ii) Creative People

No matter what the timeless qualities of the place and location, Gidleigh's success and the accolades awarded to it are the result of the hard work, dedication and creativity of the team employed here and the individuals who lead it. At the forefront of these is Michael Caines, MBE, the Executive Head Chef and a man widely regarded as one of the leading talents in British gastronomy.

Michael Caines is a busy man. He travels frequently from place to place. He has different, yet connected, business interests. His schedule is constantly hectic. Whilst some might take time to write their mission statement, you sense that Michael Caines is too busy living his mission to pause for long enough to record it. His mind races and he keeps up with it. Sometimes his sentences stop unfinished – at least, they are not always spoken to completion – as a new thought or idea is spurred forwards by the previous one. Whilst there are open fires in several of the rooms inside the house, the real fire at Gidleigh Park is Michael Caines.

His creative ambition, his need to improve constantly, is a force that did not always rest comfortably within him. It is easy to imagine that in the past the flame of his desire too often burnt rather than warmed his heart. He was, he confessed, 'always at war with myself'. Whether it was a war that could ever be won is open to question. The very nature of the creative process suggests that there can be no ultimate victory. According to Michael, 'We are in a creative and transitory industry...We are creative only for a moment...' This sense of transience continues to drive his philosophy and, in turn, his professional urgency. 'We are only here for a relatively short time,' he said once and, as he did so, his eyes glittered as if the internal fire was being refuelled, the need to fill every minute being reinforced, the willingness to accept the pain being recharged. 'I have been burnt many times and still bear the scars,' he confessed. 'But the fire within me still keeps me going. The thing that keeps my fire burning is the ability to do what I do.'

Now, however, whilst the challenges and the goals remain

the same, the internal flame is far more under control. It is, Michael reflects, the inevitable result of experience coupled with an innate desire and capability to review, identify and act upon the lessons learned. 'I am at the crossroads of life now,' he says. 'I recognise that it's not about doing more, it's about doing what you do really well.' He acknowledges, too, the obligatory costs of commitment. 'How can you value where you are if you don't endure, sacrifice or persevere?' he asks, somewhat rhetorically. 'The pain makes the pleasure more enjoyable. And we should always remember that we are privileged to be the masters of our own destiny.'

Michael has more reason than most to value the opportunities that people have to use their time in the most grateful and productive of ways. 'I nearly lost my life when I was twenty-five,' he says, the words seeming to come from deep within, 'so I see every day as a gift.'

In 1994, only a few months after taking up his role as Executive Chef at Gidleigh, Michael Caines fell asleep at the wheel of his car whilst driving home from work. In the ensuing accident he lost his right arm and almost died. In a subsequent interview Michael reflected, 'Initially, it was pretty bad and you go through days of thinking "Why me?" and "If only..." You mourn the loss of the arm, you grieve and you question your ability to go on at that point. But I was back part time at Gidleigh Park after two weeks and full time after four. I had no big insurance policy to fall back on and I thought that I was only going to find out how I could cope by getting straight back into the environment. If I came up against a barrier, I just found a new route. I took small steps that made a big difference. It was slow the first year but I regained 99.9% of what I was doing before. I had to rehabilitate myself into my surroundings using my new prosthetic arm.'

And rehabilitate himself he did. Indeed, the manner in which Michael managed both the effects of the accident and his return to work are at once inspiring and intriguing. Few can fail to be anything other than amazed and impressed by the speed of his return. Many might wonder about the motivation for such urgency. Perhaps the answer is that this is a man who could tolerate the loss of a limb more easily than he could absence from his kitchen. After all, to be out of the kitchen, to be away from Gidleigh, meant that his development and his dream were both on hold. Perhaps it also reflects the power of a personal belief system that was tested to the full and not found wanting. When asked about his ability to cope with pressure and challenge, Michael once said, 'You have to have an inner belief. I don't know where it comes from but that inner confidence has always been a part of my nature. I never really worried at school about what I'd be. I knew I'd be fine. You have to believe that what you are doing is right. You've got to have a stubbornness born of self-belief.' Perhaps, ultimately, it is just that the fire that fuels him is stronger than any single event.

Whatever the personal costs paid in full, the fire inside Michael Caines is one that draws people to him. Damien Bastiat says, 'Michael always has a queue of people wanting to work with him in the kitchen. He is driven and yet patient, and generous in many ways. He is a great teacher. He is also involved in a lot of charity work.'

However, it is for his skill as a chef and his role at Gidleigh that Michael chooses to be best known. He was born in Exeter in 1969 and adopted into what he describes as 'a large and loving family.' As a boy he used to enjoy helping in the kitchen. He recalls: 'My love of food and cooking came from the big family meals we always shared together, prepared by my mother, who was a wonderful cook. My father loved to grow vegetables and fruit in our garden, and so I grew up appreciating the flavours of the freshest foods, picked that day and simply prepared.'

It was an appreciation that turned into a career path and a commitment that became all-consuming. In later years Michael reflected, 'It's not impossible to switch off, but it is easy to be consumed by it. So you have to put yourself in situations that take your mind elsewhere. For me, when I am active doing other things, it is easy then not to think about work. Too much ambition can turn into obsession. When do you stop? At what point are you satisfied? People like Alexander the Great conquered so many lands, but it was never enough. You have to take the time to look back and appreciate what you have achieved, the distance travelled and how far you have come. When you are young you think you've got everything to prove, and as you get older you think that it doesn't matter as long as you are confident in what you are doing.'

The young Michael went to Exeter Catering College where he earned the accolade 'Student of the Year' in 1987. He then spent a year and a half at the Grosvenor House Hotel in London, before embarking on three influential years under the man he regards as his mentor, Raymond Blanc, at Le Manoir aux Quat'Saisons in Oxfordshire. From there he moved to France, training under the guidance of the late Bernard Loiseau in Saulieu and Joël Robuchon in Paris. Michael describes these men and their influence thus: 'Raymond is a visionary and a free spirit who knows no boundaries. He taught me above all to be completely open to new ideas. He has one of the best palates of any chef I've worked with. Bernard Loiseau, like Raymond, was very charismatic, larger than life. His greatest gift was the ability to extract intensity and purity of flavours from the simplest cooking, always utilising the finest local ingredients from his native Burgundy. From Loiseau, I learned the importance of regionality, something I have continued to develop here in the West Country. Joël Robuchon's technical ability was unsurpassed. A strict disciplinarian and a stern taskmaster, he sought – and demanded – precision and perfection in every way, the Swiss watchmaker of world cuisine.'

Michael returned to Britain in 1994 to take up the position of Head Chef at Gidleigh Park. It was a move that provided an enormous opportunity and challenge for such a relatively young chef. It reflected also his unswerving belief in his own creativity and skill. His self-belief was justified. In 1999 Gidleigh, with the kitchen firmly under his leadership, was awarded a second Michelin star. In 2001 Michael won Chef of the Year at the prestigious Cateys Awards. A year earlier a chance meeting with the publisher, hotelier and entrepreneur Andrew Brownsword led to a business partnership and the ongoing development of

Michael's chain of Abode hotels. In 2005 Brownsword bought Gidleigh Park for an undisclosed sum. Two years later, Michael won the AA Chefs' Chef of the Year Award. The man who had to learn how to adapt after what, for many others, would have been a career-ending injury was now established as one of the nation's greatest chefs.

When Damien Bastiat first came to England to work he could not speak a word of English. Learning the language was only one of the very significant ways he had to adapt. He explains, 'There is a very different mentality and approach in Europe when it comes to managing restaurants. In France I was used to being very assertive with my staff. It is the French way. When I moved to England I discovered that I was expected to train people and that a more measured and calm management approach was required.' Damien learnt and changed. Now he is comfortable combining leadership with staff development. 'Here,' he says, 'you are teaching whilst you are managing. Acts are more important than words. Staff learn by watching you every day.' And Damien's own education continues throughout. 'I love the people and the interactions,' he says with a controlled yet discernible sense of urgency and emotion in his voice. 'You learn as much from your guests as you do from the staff.'

Damien Bastiat is a short, wiry, clean-faced, bespectacled Frenchman. His suit fits immaculately. His shirt is perfectly pressed. His tie is perfectly knotted. His shoes shine as if new. Ask him an unexpected or, perhaps, a challenging question and he covers his pause with a gentle smile, a soft intake of breath and a slight lean away. His answer, carefully timed, will be measured as perfectly as his attire. Whilst he leads the front of house team with clarity and precision he is not, he says, the real leader at Gidleigh. That, of course, is Michael. 'Let me put it this way,' Damien explains. 'There cannot be too many leaders. It is like a sports team. There can be only one Coach in charge of everything and one Captain making it happen. Michael is the Coach. I am the Captain.'

The sporting analogy is one that both he and his Coach share with Andrew Foulkes, the General Manager. Michael talks of 'being in the zone' when working in the kitchen. Andrew is a runner and a golfer. He enjoys the sense of personal competition both activities encourage. 'I like golf because you are essentially competing against yourself,' he says. 'I see my job in the same way. Only here there are so many ways we can win. It is far more than just about achieving the bottom line. For example, I'm proud when I see a young member of the team smiling at the end of the day – that is a win!'

Andrew also values the time alone that running provides. It allows him to reflect, review and analyse. 'I take great comfort in running,' he says. 'It's my reflection time. It's when I sort out all of my problems. Once I went out for a two-mile run and came back thirteen miles later because I had a problem I couldn't solve.'

Andrew admits that he prefers to relax by doing things, by channelling his energy. 'There is a part of me that is always thinking, always analysing,' he states. 'It's relentless.' So why commit to such a demanding profession? 'Because it's an absolute passion. I love it! I want the very best for the people I work with, for every guest who comes here, for myself and my family.' And Andrew is constantly looking for ways to improve. 'Even if you are tempted to think that something is perfect,' he says, 'you know that perfection doesn't exist.'

For Damien, the creativity that leads to improvement is based on 'asking yourself constantly, "How can I, we, do this better?" It's about being very self-critical. People not used to working at this standard might find it negative because we are so critical of ourselves. Often I don't have to tell people because, if they have made a mistake, they tell themselves off. You can't expect that from people who work with you, if you don't do that yourself. It's about using customer feedback. It's about battling against yourself. Every year I say to the staff, "This is what we achieved last year – how do we do better this year?"'

Michael believes that creativity comprises a skill set that can be taught. It is not the prerogative of a gifted few. 'I think you can teach people to be creative. There are people with great ideas, but they never enact them or they are too impatient. If you have a good idea that is a sign of a good imagination, you can teach anyone how to take an idea and turn it into a practical experience. An interesting point is that in our industry there is a huge amount of logistics behind the creative process.'

It is this creative ability, Michael argues, that underpins the development of a personal and professional brand. There is, therefore, no room for compromise. 'If you dilute your own creative talent, you dilute your brand. Here it's more about me thinking about what I want to create and then making sure it is delivered well. Being creative is a process of expressing yourself. Many people can copy a great painter. Only a few rare individuals can paint the original. It's the same in the kitchen. I need my chefs to deliver with talent and care, but not to reinvent it and try to put themselves into it. I love working with my chefs,' he says. 'Just as I learned from the masters, so I hope my chefs will learn from me and continue to develop to the very best of their abilities to fulfil their potential and achieve their ambitions. We can give them this opportunity.'

Michael hopes that his chefs learn more than just the necessary skills and techniques, though. For him, the correct attitude is the foundation upon which creativity and success are built. 'You have to learn to be happy with what you are producing. You have to believe that what you are doing represents you the best. My vision as a chef is to make sure that my interpretation of what you like to eat is the best you have ever tasted. That dish is just me – it's my moment in time.' He goes on, 'If you are truly creative, there is a constant striving. Durability and endurance are so important. I'm always benchmarking. You have constantly to re-evaluate what you are doing in the marketplace without losing your values. I don't believe our industry is so special; we can learn from many things in life, but I am always saying to myself, "That's not me, so how would I do it?" Guests should be coming here because of the ways I think, not because of how others tell me I should think. When it comes down to you, your time and your calling, you have to believe that people will come to you because of your identity, your point of difference. Here at Gidleigh we are still relevant eighteen years on. It's a marathon, not a sprint.'

Michael also stresses the importance of the environment in the creative process. 'Great artists need a gallery to hang their art,' he says, 'and Gidleigh Park has become synonymous with me and I with it. I feel hugely a part of it and yet, at the same time, I'm not so attached to it that I actually need to be here. I feel at one with it. That doesn't lead to complacency, or lack of ambition. I feel very comfortable now and that brings out my creativity even more. It feels like home. I don't have negative energy here. If I was not at one with the house or it at one with me, we wouldn't be so successful.'

Andrew Foulkes, whilst acknowledging that Gidleigh 'truly is Michael's home,' talks also about the relationship between creativity and the challenges of change management. 'Like everybody I get anxiety, I get stress,' he says. 'It's about controlling that. Creativity leads to change and change is difficult sometimes. As a manager, I address the fact that people don't always like to change by explaining the reasoning behind it and by giving them time to adjust. It is important, too, to create, or develop, a strong sense of purpose within every individual. As much as possible, we want to create a synergy here so that what is good for the individual is good for the business and vice versa.'

It is a synergy that will be most easily understood and achieved by those individuals who recognise and appreciate the fact that, for as long as Michael Caines is at the forefront of Gidleigh Park, creativity will be an essential personal and corporate quality. This is not a place for people who are unwilling to be warmed by the creative fire that burns within their Executive Chef. Not surprisingly, the man who was back at work, in charge, only weeks after he nearly died has little tolerance for those who simply stand on the sidelines and critique the efforts of others.

'Personally,' he says, 'I'd rather be criticised for trying than criticise others and do nothing myself.' He goes on to develop Andrew's observation about the essential challenge of change management. 'Change is inevitably painful. Our lives are very routine. It can be an effort for some people even to try something different. So when you ask people to change it can be uncomfortable. Really creative people, though, are not comfortable with routine. They are restless. This is the difference between those who create and innovate and those who follow.' And, according to Michael, those individuals who create successful businesses also need to develop the attributes of those around them. He says, 'People who have created great businesses have done just that – they have *created* them. They are also the people who then empower others.'

When asked to sign a dinner menu Michael wrote, *After love there is only cuisine.* It is a sentiment that provides perhaps the most powerful insight into the spark that lights the flame, into his own hierarchy of beliefs and values, into why he is so driven to achieve at the highest levels, to provide food that makes the guests' journey so worthwhile. If others might challenge the relationship that Michael claims between love and cuisine, no one can doubt the importance of the relationship he shares with Gidleigh Park, the 'grand old lady'.

iii) The Lady Herself

Michael is not the only one committed to this place. Andrew Brownsword describes himself and his wife, Christina, as the 'custodians' of Gidleigh. Indeed, the way he refers to the house reinforces Damien Bastiat's emotive description. Shortly after his purchase, Andrew instigated a significant and, some might say, loving refurbishment that retained the original architectural and design influences. Originally built as a grand residential home in 1928, Gidleigh became a hotel in 1977 with fourteen bedrooms and two dining rooms. When the refurbishment was complete in December 2006, she had twenty-four bedrooms and three dining rooms, one of them incorporating a wine wall. Andrew subsequently wrote, 'Christina and I have had a love affair with Gidleigh Park and this little corner of heaven in Devon for many years... The house has certainly settled into her new persona... Christina and I will continue to add to the personality of the house.'

The 2006 additions include a wing of bedrooms with stunning bathrooms. In one there is a sauna, another has a hot tub on its own private balcony, and the spa suite has its own steam room and sauna with a private balcony overlooking the valley. The purpose here and throughout the house is to provide a seductively cosy mix of comfort, luxury and timelessness. All public rooms and bedrooms are individually furnished with antiques and fine English fabrics. There are log fires burning every day of the year, and cut flowers brighten every room.

The seductive nature of the house does not only influence the many guests who return wanting to spend as much time as possible within the place, wanting to be at Gidleigh rather than use it as a base from which to travel; it also appeals to staff. Andrew Foulkes first saw Gidleigh Park on the front cover of the 1996 Johansen Guide. He felt an immediate attraction and applied to work here as a chef. When that was unsuccessful he applied again in his gap year. Unfortunately, there were no opportunities available, but Michael Caines did phone him to discuss his application and his interest. Neither man could have known that the next time Andrew applied it would be for a very different role. 'When I was shortlisted for this job,' Andrew recalls, 'my hardest interview was with Michael. It was a really intensive two and a half hours!'

It is an intensity that is kept well away from guests. For them, the experience is designed to be far more tranquil. Those visiting Gidleigh for the first time enter the house to discover that there is no reception desk here. Instead, the front door opens into an entrance hall that is at once homely and magnificent, welcoming and refined. To your left a log fire dominates the wall. There are the smells of burning wood and fresh flowers. It is the first indication that the nature of the outside world is brought inside whilst still keeping guests warm and comfortable.

It is a reminder, too, that you have just entered a house, a home, rather than a stereotypical hotel. At Gidleigh, once you have found your way you truly have arrived. There are no tangible barriers that you have to pass through. In most hotels the reception is a form of no-man's-land. It is the space you have to traverse before you feel that you have been accepted in. In most hotels the reception is an area designed to enable the processing of occupants and the movement of visitors. It is the part of the establishment that separates those who are staying from those who are just passing through and yet it is available to both. Here, though, there is quite literally an entrance: an introduction to a change of state, a shift inwards in the most positive of ways. Somehow Gidleigh surrounds her guests with both herself and the wider, natural environment. The link between the two is perhaps most obviously reflected in the locally sourced food that is at the heart of Michael Caines' cuisine.

Diners are encouraged to sit in the lounge before they eat. The room provides another fire and more flowers. During the day there are great views over the gardens and the valley and at night a darkness that is deliberately unlit, reminding everyone that they are on the moor, reinforcing both the isolation of the house and the comfort it offers.

There are three dining rooms, all off the main corridor that runs from the entrance hall. In each room tables are well spaced. Guests are meant to feel at home. They are meant to experience a sense of timelessness. No matter how brief their stay at Gidleigh everything – the setting, the house, the service and the food – is intended to make it feel as if time has stopped. The 'Gidleigh Way', as staff refer to it, is to offer guests peacefulness and excellence. It is to encourage them to focus on the *now* of their current experience, to be remote and yet connected, to be removed from their daily obligations and thus given the opportunity to be reminded of, and reconnect with, those things that matter most in their life.

Menus include a seasonal set lunch, à la carte, a vegetarian and two tasting options, one of which offers a selection of Michael's most famous dishes. The food reflects his classic French training and his creativity, and it offers another example of the relationship between what happens inside Gidlegh and the environment. This time, though, it is an environment beyond the moor. It is the sea.

Michael wrote, 'As chefs, in recent years, we have had to become far more aware of our responsibilities to the environment. One area that we chefs especially need to be aware of is the sustainability of the food produce and products that we use. Great ingredients are necessary to the creation of great food, so we need to ensure that what we are using today will be sustainable and therefore available for the chefs of tomorrow and the future. Fish and seafood is an important example. Over-fishing is widely acknowledged to be an immense threat to marine wildlife and fish habitats.

'Many of our own fish stocks are in a state of serious decline. So then, what can we all do? We need to be aware above all of the provenance of the fish we use and wherever possible purchase fish sourced from responsibly managed fisheries. Often it's not just a question of the type of fish or shellfish, but how it has been caught or gathered from the sea. Scallops picked up off the seabed by divers may be more sustainable than those gathered by trawlers. Sea bass that is line-caught is preferable to that which is netted by the larger trawlers.

'Demand often fuels over-fishing...so consumers need to become more adventurous and seek greater variety. Fish such as red gurnard, hake, wild sea trout, black bream, and pollack are all fish that may be less valued than more widely touted varieties, and so serve as more sustainable alternatives. I urge you when choosing fish to try something new – it may not just be better for the marine environment, it will also help to broaden your taste and you may discover some delicious new flavours.'

Michael and his team develop personal relationships with the fishermen, farmers, butchers and artisan food producers who supply them. All share the belief that sustainability and traceability are key links in the conservation chain, and that good food really matters.

At Gidleigh the much-better-than-good food is supported by a wine cellar regarded as one of the very best in the country. Housing around eleven hundred bins, the cellar was another part of Andrew Brownsword's refurbishment project. Approximately ten thousand bottles are stored in perfect conditions. The man responsible for managing this selection and ensuring that guests enjoy a wine that complements their food perfectly is Master Sommelier Edouard Oger.

Edouard is a softly-spoken Frenchman who grew up in the Loire Valley. His uncle was a wine maker and Edouard spent much of his time with him in the vineyard. He recalls, 'I knew straight away that I wanted to be in the wine business, but not in the vineyard. I needed to have people around me. I really like to meet people and I have always loved serving people. So I thought I can become either a bar manager or a sommelier.' He chose the latter, and set his sights on achieving the highest qualification and status possible, that of Master Sommelier. It required a lengthy and rigorous period of study.

Edouard explains, 'The Master Sommelier programme is for people who want to sell and serve wine. The qualification is seen to be as high as a Master in Wine, but the focus is very different even though both programmes are knowledge-based. The training on the Master Sommelier programme is very stressful. You are under pressure because they can ask you anything about any wine they want, whether it is from France, Italy, Spain, Croatia, Uruguay, anywhere! You have to study pretty much every day. The blind tasting is the most stressful part. You are given six wines, three red and three white, and through taste alone you have to be able to identify the country, the region, the grape and also the vintage. You have only twenty-five minutes to do this. It is so stressful that I have been physically sick before every testing. I have always managed to be successful, though.'

Edouard goes on, 'A Sommelier is not someone who spends a bit of time on the floor serving people and the rest of their time in the vineyard. We spend our time mainly here on the floor helping people, making sure that they have a great time... The Sommelier is very important because if you have a great dish in front of you and you have with it a great wine it becomes magical!'

To be able to recommend the best wine to accompany every dish, Edouard not only needs to be knowledgeable about the wine in his cellar; he also needs to understand Michael's cuisine. He says, 'I have to understand the food completely. Which is not to say that I can tell you as much about it as Damien – he understands absolutely everything – but I do taste the food and get to know the flavours, the textures and structures, because if I don't know this I cannot recommend the best wine match.'

Despite his qualification as a Master Sommelier and his commitment to furthering his knowledge, Edouard has not yet managed to taste every wine in Gidleigh's extensive list. He confesses, with just a hint of unnecessary embarrassment, 'I know over nine hundred of our wines very well. However, there are fifty or so that I have not tasted yet. These wines I have only read about.'

For Edouard the desire to continue learning is matched only by the need to match the excellence of Michael's kitchen brigade and Damien's front of house team in the pursuit of creating something magical. It is a pursuit without end, one that cannot be measured in weeks, months or even years. Paradoxically, though, the magic they seek to create is dependent upon exceptional time management.

iv) Clockwise

Systems that gather and share customer information and record and manage timings are at the heart of the Gidleigh operation. The operation is designed to run like clockwork. There are four wall clocks in the kitchen, each showing exactly the same time. A fifth clock, matching the timing of the other four, is on Damien's desk at the heart of front of house operations. Everything is written down and shared amongst staff. Everything is checked three times for accuracy.

Damien explains, 'The guests arrive and are welcomed at the door or outside. They are shown to the lounge where they are given the menus and wine list to read. We record both where they sat and the time they sat down. From then we have half an hour for them to relax before we take them through to the restaurant. Within that time canapés are prepared and guests will receive these within ten minutes of sitting down. We give them five minutes to enjoy these and then I will go and take the menu order. We allocate five minutes for this. Following this, Edouard will need five or six minutes per table to take their wine order. That leaves guests with four or five minutes more to enjoy their time in the lounge and then we invite them through to the restaurant.

'The aim is to do all of this in that time without rushing them or making them feel that they are waiting. To do this we need to be organised and you also need to know how to read people, to know their purpose for being here, their scheduling. I have to get these things right for the sake of both the guests and the kitchen. I have to avoid putting the kitchen team under too much pressure. For the guests it all has to seem like a natural flow. The example I always use with my staff is that of the air hostess. If you ever see the hostess running to the cockpit you know that something is wrong. So no matter what pressure we might be feeling, we have to make it seem effortless, calm and fine.

'It is important that everyone understands the chain of command. Everything you do impacts on other people. So we have a system in which we aim to bring a table of two through to the restaurant every five minutes, a table of four every ten minutes. We know we can cope with this because we have a total of fifty covers and we can manage eight to ten every thirty minutes.

'Everything is reported and recorded. We record what time the drinks order is taken, what time the canapés are served, when the menu order and the wine order are taken. Then we record what time the guests are taken through to their table. After that, we aim for the first course to be served within ten to fifteen minutes. When that is finished, it's then fifteen to twenty minutes before the main course is served. Getting timings right is at the heart of managing the guests' dining experience.'

When asked to describe the place where he works, Damien struggles for words more obviously than at any other time. Finally, he says, 'I think Gidleigh is beautiful. It is… timeless.' He considers briefly and then adds, 'Even though we are always looking at the clock.'

There are regular Head-of-Department meetings and a staff briefing before each service. There is a focus, too, on training to ensure the development of individual and team performance.

Andrew says, 'My role involves a mixture of strategising and developing the people in the teams at every level. I want everyone here to be the very best they can be.'

Edouard cascades learning through his team. 'I train Clio, my assistant,' he explains, 'and then she trains the other two.'

The capability of individual staff is not the only – perhaps not even the primary – requirement. According to Damien, 'This is not just a job, it's a lot more than that. You have to love what you are doing. We are facing guests sixteen or seventeen hours a day. If you don't love this the guests will feel it. We have to train our staff and also we have to recognise those who do not have it.'

As Executive Chef, and with his own chain of hotels and restaurants to develop, Michael is at Gidleigh only two or three days each week. For the most part, then, he provides leadership from long distance. Damien is, quite literally, his eyes and ears. The two men understand each other extremely well and both recognise the importance of the other. Damien is clear about his priorities: he serves Gidleigh, Michael Caines and his customers. Although the three are inextricably linked, he speaks of them always in this order. Michael is his leader and, as far as Damien is concerned, he is the leader of Gidleigh Park. Andrew Brownsword owns the business. Michael Caines is the inspiration who shapes and grows the business.

Damien says, 'Respect is one thing you can never get just by asking for it. And Michael has a hell of a lot of respect here. I don't know how he does it, being here only a few days a week.'

It is a point reinforced readily by Operations Manager, Scott Andrews. 'When you work with someone like Michael,' he says, 'you realise that he just has a natural ability to inspire others. It's difficult to explain what it is about him or how he does it. It's not something you can put into words easily.'

There is clarity, though, about the responsibility that Damien, Scott and the other managers have during Michael's absence. Damien explains, 'Our job is to ensure that whilst he is away standards are maintained. When he isn't here, Michael and I will call each other, or email. He is always available. He never really switches off.'

According to Michael, the fact that standards are maintained is a mark of organisational effectiveness. 'The success of any business is its ability to continue in your absence,' he explains. 'You need to be able to get your staff to think and act like you, so they can manage things when you are not there. I'm a control freak in many regards. I don't like to let go of things until I have the right outcome. Because I have great systems in place at Gidleigh, I can let it go and not be there all the time. Systems are the most important things. Systems and personal discipline.'

It is easy to imagine that it took time for both Michael and the staff to become comfortable and confident in this situation. Now, though, the sometimes long-distant leader is clearly at home with the arrangement and with its value as a key measure of organisational capability.

When taking bookings, staff are required to find out guests' reasons for visiting and any special requirements they might have. This is regarded as the first step in ensuring that individual needs can be identified and met and that all guests enjoy a personalised experience when visiting Gidleigh.

Marketing focuses on the unique selling points of the business, specifically the restaurant and reputation of Michael Caines, the house itself and its unique location. Michael makes the point, 'Many great brands are either names of people or they are synonymous with a person... It's the people who make a business successful, having a common focus and purpose, a real team spirit in pursuit of excellence.' Whilst his name is synonymous with Gidleigh, another powerful form of marketing stems from the many awards that both the house and the restaurant have won over the years. For example, in 2009 Gidleigh Park was awarded 'Hotel of the Year' at the Enjoy England Awards for Excellence. In 2010 the restaurant came first in the *Sunday Times* survey of the best one hundred restaurants in the UK. And one year later Condé Nast Johansens voted Gidleigh Park the 'Most Excellent Restaurant' in their 2011 Excellence Awards.

The many accolades reflect Michael Caines's philosophy that, 'It's about standing out, not fitting in.' Gidleigh Park, though, does both in equal measure. Whilst standing out as a picture of excellence, acknowledged as such by significant peers and critics, Gidleigh is inescapably a picture that is forever framed by the beauty of an environment and a landscape that offers its very own magic. All around the house, nature displays its own creativity, shares its own structure and systems, celebrates change and, at times, covers the ground with its own unique confetti. Here the frame is at least as picturesque and emotive as that which it surrounds. Indeed, it is easy to argue that only the most creative individuals could produce and maintain something worthy of such enclosure.

To understand Gidleigh, both its personality and success, one has to understand the relationship it shares with, and the influence of, the environment that frames it. It is impossible to imagine one without the other.

v) Nature's Confetti

Damien Bastiat once said, 'Gidleigh is a special place. It has an effect on us.' The effect that he refers to is created by more than just the house alone: it is a result of another type of synergy – that which exists between the building and the setting, between the natural environment and the man-made one.

Since 1995 the estate has grown in size from its previous forty-seven acres to over one hundred. The many developments include the introduction of additional walks along the river banks, through the bluebell wood and the woodland itself. Within the estate there is a large terraced herb garden, which supplies the kitchen with fresh herbs, fruit and vegetables; a number of flowerbeds, an 18-hole putting course, two croquet lawns, a tennis court and a bowling green.

When asked what guests are purchasing when they visit Gidleigh, Scott Andrews replied immediately, 'They are getting an unrivalled location with the grounds and the National Park. Without a doubt this is a stunning place in a stunning location. Of course, they are also getting the chance to experience one of the very finest restaurants. Michael's food is ever-evolving. And then there is the staff and the quality of service. There are other brilliant restaurants to eat in throughout the country, but often when you leave them you step out into the street. Here you step out into the estate and gardens, and, if you want, into the moor.'

The refurbishment of Gidleigh in 2006 provided the inspiration for the current herb garden. When a vast supply of Dartmoor granite was discovered within the site, it was decided that it should be recycled into the development. A team of local craftsmen was employed to create the granite terraces that now form the garden walls. The team used the traditional techniques of dry-stone walling to achieve their task, sometimes having to manoeuvre boulders weighing over half a ton. Apart from when there is such exceptional work to be done, the estate is managed on a day-to-day basis by a team of four gardeners. The grounds are designed to be beautiful, relaxing and functional. Guests can book a 'Grounds and Gardens' tour, which incorporates an hour's tour of the gardens followed by lunch. Those guests who want to spend more time in the open air are ideally placed, for they are surrounded by a protected world of ebb and flow, of history and legend, of isolation and industry.

Beyond the estate, Dartmoor itself stretches for over three hundred and sixty square miles. Here the invitation to write your own story is writ large and the more you want to, the moor will help you.

The gardens extend from the house down into the valley. The moor is out of sight, beyond woodland. Guests are offered a choice of mapped walks taking anything from two to five hours to complete. They all start and end at the house. The moor is reached by walking first through the water garden. This offers another example of how Gidleigh is designed and managed to fit into its location. The water garden is created to appear wild, to provide a seamless transition between the traditional gardens of the house and the wilderness of the moor. In autumn coloured leaves cover the path like nature's confetti.

The moor takes its name from the river Dart which flows across and beyond it, finally reaching the sea at Dartmouth. Capped with many exposed granite hilltops known as tors, Dartmoor includes the largest area of granite in Britain and is rich in antiquities and archaeology. The high ground forms the catchment area for many of Devon's rivers. These play their part not only in shaping the landscape, but also as power sources for such traditional moorland industries as tin mining and quarrying. On a far more ethereal level Dartmoor is a storehouse of myths and legends, and has inspired such writers as Sir Arthur Conan Doyle and Agatha Christie.

Although it is protected by National Park status, much of the moor has been designated as 'Access Land', meaning that whilst it may be privately owned, there are no restrictions on where walkers can roam. There are also over four hundred and fifty miles of public rights of way and myriad footpaths and bridleways where the owners allow access.

Many of the walks provide stunning views and all add further to the sense of timelessness that Gidleigh seeks to create. They offer the most natural form of exercise, combining tranquillity and effort, as a complement to the luxury and comfort of the house. As one guest remarked, 'It is even cosier inside once you have walked on the moor.'

The isolation of the house, whilst attractive to guests, limits the social options available to staff when they are not working. As Scott observes, those who seek employment here do so purely for professional reasons. 'If you are going to work in a property like this, which is so removed from the big cities, you are going to do so because you really want to achieve. Staff really are here because they want to be. We all have our different reasons for being at Gidleigh, but we are all focused on the same thing, which is providing the very highest quality experience for our guests.'

The quality of that experience is greatly influenced and enhanced by the setting and the landscape. However much guests might appreciate the warmth and comfort of the house upon their arrival, they value it anew when they return from having spent time on the moor. It is a warmth that is created as much by the staff as it is by the building itself. Damien says, 'Gidleigh allows you to be the host of the hotel. All staff, irrespective of status, behave towards the guests as if they are the host of the hotel.'

By way of contrast the moor has no host. It offers contrasts rather than guarantees. It gives visitors the chance to be reminded of something far more basic, more primal, than modern-day luxury. If, as Michael Caines believes, systems are most important then the moor is the most important of all. It is the result of a myriad of systems working together to create an environment that supports and sustains both wildlife and people, industry and escapism. It is at once a record of the past and a vital measure of the present. It is a living, changing location with as many different faces as a crowd. And Gidleigh Park, that fine old lady, is one of the most memorable.

vi) Location, Location, Location

The adage 'It doesn't matter what you know, but who you know' might have a twin that reads 'It doesn't just matter who you are, it also matters where you are.' When we talk about where we are, we are inevitably revealing both location and time. The story of Gidleigh Park and the creative, purposeful people who are committed to working there is, in one sense, also a story about space and time management.

Michael Caines is clear that 'what I am very good at doing is seeing space and turning it into a successful business reality.' Creative people develop new, more relevant ways to fill space and use time. When Michael states, 'If what you offer is not seen as relevant, if it doesn't fit, people won't buy it,' he is talking about a 'fit' in both time and space. The innovative offering has to fit current needs and be located appropriately. The successful application of creative processes depends upon great timing, great placement and great communication. To ensure that others value their innovation, creative people have to share their vision in a timely and persuasive fashion. They have to create a space for themselves in the marketplace and then draw their required audience to them. The draw has to be so great that people will even follow a narrow, winding road in pursuit of the benefits on offer.

This creative management of time and space begins with a vision. Michael is in no doubt that 'having a vision and then not sharing it is probably the biggest waste of talent there is.' The vision has to be given life and maintained through the logistics and systems that Michael holds dear. The new reality also has to fit within its environment and be 'of its time'. The implication is that, sooner or later, its time will pass and, unless there has been both re-evaluation and regrowth, its value will be lost.

Interestingly, the story of Gidleigh Park introduces the notion that creative change exists around a set of unchanging corporate values. One of the skills of the creative person, then, would seem to be distinguishing what can be changed from what cannot, being able to answer the question, 'How do we adapt over time and yet remain true to our essential identity and purpose?'

Whilst Michael Caines is certain that creative skills and processes can be taught, whether the same can be said for the appropriate underpinning attitudes is open to debate. Michael's inner confidence, his willingness to strive continually for improvement, the importance he places on 'stubbornness born of self-belief', are all, by his own admission, an inherent part of his psychological make-up. He does admit, however, that some of his attitudes have changed as a result of experience. There is a very clear sense that the man who said, 'You have to learn to be happy with what you are doing' did, actually, have to learn how to feel that way. Perhaps the inner flame that fuels Michael was within him from birth, perhaps it was strengthened by events. What is evident, though, is that he has learned how to control and direct it. Now the chef who recognises and is motivated by the fact that 'we are creative only for a moment', who is wedded to the belief that we are all masters of our own destiny, seems to be as comfortable managing his own energy and zeal as he is in his relationship with Gidleigh Park.

The relationship between creativity, adaptability and change management is an intimate one. Corporate creativity often leads to a change in systems and structures, a change in staff behaviours and required skills. Such changes can, as Andrew Foulkes acknowledged, lead to feelings of stress and anxiety. Indeed, Andrew talked of being frequently out of his 'comfort zone'. Yet he described himself as 'the luckiest person in the world.' Again, for those individuals who welcome change and its associated challenges, a creative environment provides the inspiration for personal and professional growth. For those who favour routine and the certainty of repetition this is clearly not the case. The creative people at the heart of Gidleigh Park lead by example. They demonstrate the desired behaviours and attitudes, teaching by actions as well as words. Here, in this somewhat isolated place, there is no room for people who do not want to embrace the creative culture, to stoke the fires of meaningful, balanced change continually.

The way the relative isolation of Gidleigh influences recruitment is just one example of how powerfully the location impacts upon the business. As Scott Andrews noted, the staff who are drawn here are attracted by their desire to learn from, and become a part of, the Gidleigh Way. The road leading up to the house, the gardens and estate, the wildness and complexity of the moor, all play their own significant parts in influencing that Way. The storybook nature of Gidleigh and the experience it offers, the sign encouraging travellers to 'Keep heart', the welcome above the door that reads 'Once upon a time', are all in keeping with a landscape that has inspired some of our greatest writers and storytellers.

The décor inside the house, creating the sense of a warm, luxurious home rather than a high-tech hotel, is as much a consequence of the natural environment that surrounds it, as of the structure and style of the building itself. This is a place where families can sit together in the lounge and play board games, where individuals can find a comfy chair and just sit and read, where there is an ever-present invitation just to look out at the gardens and the valley beyond, to feel cosy and cosseted especially when the weather is bleak or the night pulls down an impenetrable darkness.

The emphasis on locally-sourced food also reinforces the relationship between Gidleigh and her location. It emphasises, too, the pride that Michael Caines has in his local region. His comments about the dangers of over-fishing reveal a concern for an environment that, at first glance, appears to be far removed from Gidleigh and her place on the moor. More significantly, though, it reinforces his awareness of the importance of systems and the way they can stretch across, and connect, different environments.

Michael's long-distance leadership is another example of organisational and strategic stretch. The fact that he does not always need to be present for his influence and authority to be felt is due to the power of his personal charisma, the ability of the senior managers and his constant communication with them, and the appropriateness of the systems in place. The fact that he is not always there also provides two very specific benefits. It encourages Michael to see the house and all that is taking place within her afresh. It offers the clarity of perspective that is difficult to maintain on a daily basis when the habit of routine and repetition can blind leaders to certain realities, tricking them into seeing only what they expect to. Michael's time away also emphasises and develops the sense of trust that has to exist between all involved. In this regard the staff have to be as certain of Michael's continual commitment to Gidleigh despite his absence as he is of their ability to maintain standards without him. It can be argued that trust that is rewarded plays a powerful role in building positive relationships and holding them together. This might, in turn, help to explain further the quality of the dynamic between Michael and the team.

The final very obvious lesson we can take from Gidleigh Park is about the importance of effective time management. This is dependent upon far more than simply having systems in place to manage time. It is about the ability to set and achieve the most appropriate deadlines, whilst ensuring that everyone understands how important this is in the creation of a magical experience. It is this shared realisation that underpins the very effective and efficient staff interactions, particularly within and between the front of house and kitchen teams. This interactivity, intended to go unnoticed by the guests, is the foundation for the apparently effortless, yet extremely timely service, for the exceptional standard of the food, for the timeless quality of the Gidleigh Park Way.

It is a way that is founded upon the coexistence of a range of opposites, a bringing together of what might be regarded as Yin and Yang forces with the intention of creating the perfect whole. The first of these is the fact that the tranquillity and timelessness of the guests' experience is dependent upon great timekeeping by the staff. The second is the comfort of the house surrounded by the wildness of the moor, each emphasising the unique nature of the other. Thirdly, we realise that here is a house with a history that has been developed and refurbished to encourage and enable an appreciation of *now*, of the pure enjoyment of living in the moment without thoughts of past or future. And, finally, there is the outward-inward nature of the experience. It is an experience based upon the guests' willingness to travel, to Gidleigh in the first instance and then into the house, or out into the estate or the moor before returning back for the comfort and the food and the service. Ultimately, then, no matter how much a guest might travel out, the journey here ends on an inward route, as Gidleigh gently leads the way into whatever altered, peaceful state the guest is seeking.

When Edouard Oger was asked to explain his personal philosophy in the light of his own experiences and the lessons he has learnt from those around him, particularly Michael Caines, he thought for a moment and then replied simply, 'Everything is possible as long as you want it enough.' And perhaps at Gidleigh Park everything really is.

2

Knowing Who You Are: Le Manoir aux Quat'Saisons, Oxfordshire

'I found my passion'

Raymond Blanc OBE

Introduction

This is a story about vision, belief and ownership. It highlights the importance of having a clear sense of identity, and of combining macro- and micro-management. It is a story about how to create and manage a learning organisation and, most importantly, it is a story about passion and how to share it with others to create something special.

The story of Le Manoir aux Quat'Saisons offers lessons about:
- The power of an emotive, clear and detailed vision
- The role of recruitment and selection in maintaining and developing organisational culture and the implementation of strategy
- The value of ensuring that every individual understands and appreciates every aspect of the organisation's operations
- The relationship and inevitable tension between idealism and commercial necessity
- The characteristics and benefits of a learning organisation
- Charismatic, transformational leadership.

i) Out of the Soil

Le Manoir aux Quat'Saisons, quite literally the house of four seasons, stands next to the church in the sleepy, picturesque Oxfordshire village of Great Milton. Whilst the church is intended to draw the visitors' thoughts and eyes heavenward, the experience offered at Le Manoir is more firmly rooted in the soil.[1] Beautifully tended lawns, flower borders and orchards lead to a two-acre *jardin potager*, a kitchen garden which provides an amazing array of vegetables and herbs. Apart from the delights of the Tea Garden, the Apple Orchard and the Malaysian Garden, which won a silver medal at the 2005 Chelsea Flower Show, the potager produces ninety different types of vegetable and over seventy varieties of herb, all of which find their way, via the kitchen, onto the diners' plates. A range of European and Oriental leaf crops are grown to add variety to the salads offered. The soil itself is managed organically and in August 2000 the gardens at Le Manoir achieved full organic status from the Soil Association. It is an achievement that is valued greatly by the man who is the leader of, and inspiration behind, Le Manoir aux Quat'Saisons: Raymond Blanc.

RB, as he is affectionately called by all of his staff, first saw a photograph of the house in a copy of *Country Life* magazine in 1982. The house was for sale and it appealed to him instantly. That very same day, having discovered that the current owner was Lady Cromwell, Raymond drove to Great Milton. In his autobiography, *A Taste of My Life,* he describes his first reaction upon seeing the house.

'I was in awe. It was something from the pages of Lewis Carroll: the mini-grand gravel driveway, the large creaking gates, the immaculate lawns, the old walls, the caramel-yellow Oxford stone, the grand little house topped with four chimney stacks... If anything, it looked a little severe, a little masculine: maybe a small statement about the vanity and power of man. I would add the feminine touch...'

---

1 Although guests might well argue that, whilst the gardens do indeed draw their attention to the soil, the food itself is heavenly!

The house had been built in 1356 by a Frenchman called Aginscourt; now, hundreds of years later, it was about to return to French hands. Lady Cromwell supported Raymond's intention to turn the manor house into a hotel and restaurant and championed his cause amongst the local population. On 17 March 1984, having secured a government grant and attracted additional investment, Raymond invited guests into Le Manoir aux Quat'Saisons for the very first time. Even then his vision was clear and the gardens were at the centre of it.

'I wanted to create a level of excellence you couldn't find in Britain. I was not just thinking of the cuisine, though I knew that had to be good. I was also thinking about creating a wonderful garden and grounds... I was thinking of having a cookery school, too, where home cooks would discover the pure joy and creative act of cooking. This had to be a great hotel and restaurant where people could come and celebrate. I wanted the greatest eating place in the world. I wanted conviviality – happy staff and happy guests. People, after all, are at the very heart of a restaurant's success.'

And the plan was that the restaurant would be stocked as much as possible by the garden produce. However, this would require endless hard work and creativity. When Raymond first bought Le Manoir the lawn was magnificent and the vegetable garden was completely overgrown, lacking any sign of cultivation or care. It was the complete opposite of the garden he had known at home as a child in France. There his father spent most of his free time expertly tending a massive potager, whilst showing little interest in their tiny lawn. Not surprisingly, then, Raymond was introduced to gardening as a young boy. At first he hated it, although over the years his attitude changed dramatically. He recalls precisely how his father first emphasised to him the importance of the soil. It was a lesson that the young Raymond did not appreciate at the time and yet came to value with a passion. He was seven years old when, '...My father scooped out some earth and showed it to me. He made me look at it, smell it, even taste it. That way, he said, I would know how things would grow in it. Smelling and looking would show whether it was a clay soil or limy; tasting... I think my father got carried away.'

Decades later the boy who was required to taste soil talks about the vital importance of the earth in the production of great food with the certainty, energy and enthusiasm of a man who has long been committed to working the land, who understands nature and seeks to manage it productively, who has a passion and a philosophy that are both made manifest in the gardens he has created. When Raymond Blanc talks of how great produce comes 'out of the soil', he is reminding us of the need to address the first things first, quite literally to do the groundwork that underpins the creation of quality and the capability of sustainable growth. He is reminding us of the need to care for, and work with, nature whilst also reflecting the determination of his kitchen and gardening teams to ensure a direct synergy between what goes into and comes out of the soil and what appears in his restaurant.

In one sense everything at Le Manoir reflects something of Raymond Blanc and yet the gardens, the way they look, the ways they are managed and developed, the different ways they impact upon the guests' experience, perhaps more than anything else reveal something about the attitudes, the values – even the soul – of this self-taught chef, restaurateur, hotelier and industry leader. It is easy to see his transformation of the gardens through what might be called a process of controlled collaboration with nature as the ideal metaphor for the way he has returned a most-welcome French influence into this most-English part of the countryside, for the way he leads his staff and ensures their constant interactions with each other, and for how he relates to the media and searches continually for an ever-higher standard of excellence whilst always remaining true to his roots.

Anne Marie Owens, the Head Gardener at Le Manoir, who has worked with Raymond since 1985 when her summer job turned into a permanent position, believes that if he had not become a chef he would have been a gardener. That might well be so. However, since he first bought the house, Raymond has cultivated more than just the land and produced more than just the vegetables and herbs his guests enjoy. He has grown a business that combines the deliberate management of nature, buildings, people and media to provide what appears to be effortless luxury throughout the year.

The changing seasons direct the changes in the menus, activities and experiences that all guests can enjoy. The House for all Seasons reflects the cyclic nature of life through a combination of the profoundly simplistic acceptance of what nature offers at any given time, and the strategic and creative capabilities of the highly skilled and completely committed human beings who work there. No matter what the time of year, the gardens serve their multi-layered role continually. They serve and influence the menus, and they play a crucial role in establishing and reinforcing the identity of the place and the business, providing relaxation, education and inspiration for the guests.

The gardens do far more than bring together a French influence in the English countryside; they are global in their reach. Here a mushroom valley, home to an incredible variety of fungi, is within easy walking distance of a Japanese garden. More than a dozen varieties of beetroot are grown within sight of a wide range of Southeast Asian produce and an apple orchard. Here France-in-England incorporates the rest of the world in pursuit of a timeless luxury that makes the most of the inevitability of change. And the garden's influence extends beyond the kitchen and the restaurant. Bedroom names and designs reflect the microclimates and the cultures contained within the grounds. Rooms titled Lemongrass, Jade and Opium highlight the Asian connection and Rouge et Noir, Provence and Manon are amongst those which reinforce the French. Whether guests visit Le Manoir in spring, autumn, summer or winter, the gardens play their significant role both inside and outside the buildings.

And it was Raymond's father who played a significant role in helping to organise and establish the gardens. For the first six months of his ownership Raymond worked tirelessly to create a semblance of order within the grounds, to lay the foundation for his great plan, for the cultivation of value and beauty. When he began, the potager was, he says, '...overgrown with ground elder and dead Brussels sprouts. What vegetables there were had been devoured by the rabbits, which were everywhere. A garden that is not cultivated turns into a forest. My heart sank a little when I first saw it, but I recognised it as an opportunity.' Just tackling the problem was, he admits, 'a massive task'. However, by the time his parents arrived the process of tidying up the vegetable garden and re-energising the soil was complete. With the help of his father, who had brought with him a variety of seeds for planting, and accompanied by Albert Ring, an experienced gardener, and apprentice Anne Marie, Raymond pushed ahead with the transformation. Unlike his childhood days in the potager, he acknowledges that this time, 'I was the one doing the delegating and he (my father) was the one getting his hands dirty.'

Unfortunately, the garden not only needed to be cultivated; it also needed to be reclaimed from the rabbits. Raymond still remembers the devastation they caused and the desolation he felt. 'Every morning I would visit my beloved young vegetables and herbs and one day I was devastated by the sight that greeted me. Overnight, the entire garden had been chomped by rabbits. I knew the rabbits were a problem, but there was so much damage done in one night that I was convinced Le Manoir's rabbits must have brought their hungry friends and family from elsewhere... I put a huge pile of cabbage in the grounds and erected a sign which read, "That's for you, rabbits." It didn't work. They just ate the cabbage, and then everything else.'

Eventually the problem was resolved by a piece of very specific planting. An expensive rabbit-resistant fence was erected around the potager and secured deep underground to prevent burrowing. Raymond's father then provided and planted more seeds that grew over time to serve the kitchen rather than the wildlife.

Nowadays the only eating done in the garden is by guests enjoying an informative guided tour and by the chefs tasting the produce. Anne Marie describes these times when chefs taste, discuss and consider new culinary possibilities as being 'inevitably creative. The kitchen team are always exploring ideas for new dishes and combinations and, often, they will ask us (the garden team) questions we did not expect and have never considered. For example, I was asked once if the bark from a particular tree was edible!' Anne Marie is certain that 'this willingness we have to explore and experiment, and the close working relationship between the kitchen and garden teams play a huge part in creating the standards that are associated with Le Manoir.'

Sometimes, Anne Marie admits, there can also be a degree of tension in the air, particularly when chefs are tasting the very latest produce and 'RB is stood back, silently, watching, listening to their opinions before he offers his own.'

The creativity Anne Marie describes extends beyond the cooking of the garden produce to include the growing of it. Variations of well-established vegetables and herbs are developed and grown, sometimes, for example, with the intention of creating a miniature version that will look better on a plate and have a more intense flavour. Now, after years of experimentation, lemongrass and other Southeast Asian herbs are grown all year round.

The gardens at Le Manoir have changed enormously since 1984 so, one might ask, has Raymond Blanc's original vision been achieved? The answer would appear to be both 'Yes' and 'No'. His aim to create and combine luxury with standards of excellence at every turn, and a synergy between the grounds and the house, has clearly been met. However, here the search for improvement is as continual as the changing of the seasons. The soil might have full organic status and yet neither the gardens nor the business grow purely organically. They are shaped, shifted and progressed through a continual desire to become ever better. The quest to discover what lies on the other side of excellence is one, it seems, from which there is no return.

Perhaps the answer to the question does lie within the soil. Perhaps it is to be found within the hearts and minds of creative human beings. Either way, the collaboration with nature that is at the core of Le Manoir aux Quat'Saisons continues to inspire guests and staff alike, and to reveal insights into the values of their leader, the self-confessed idealist.

ii) The Idealist and the Compromise

Raymond Blanc is a man of unprepossessing stature, with an expressive, emotive face. However, it would be an error when describing this man to focus on his physicality. Only the most astute observer would pass him by on the street and recognise the deep well of energy from which he draws his enthusiasm. It is, though, only ever just below the surface. The briefest of conversations quickly brings it to the fore. He is a man used to talking to the media. He has stories that he shares, ideologies that he promotes, lines that he takes. He tells them all with intensity in his eyes and sometimes a faraway look when recalling an experience, with gestures of his hands that one moment appear to be holding or shaping with care and then to be searching for something just out of reach. As he warms to his subject, he gives the sense that he is somehow tasting the words before he delivers them.

Raymond Blanc has a charisma that can be neither taught nor learnt. He wears his passion like a well-cut suit. It is impossible to separate the man from his vision and purpose. There is no gap between what he says and what he does – and what he expects from the people he employs. It is easy to believe that the never-ending immediacy of his chosen profession is the perfect motivating force for him. The food and hospitality that he offers are, quite literally, consumed within the instant; they disappear as they are enjoyed. Think of an artist, a great painter, who wakens each morning knowing that he will find his canvas blank, that no matter how beautiful his artistry yesterday, it has already vanished forever. And the sight of that blank canvas, the opportunities it offers, the chance for constant reinvention, is the reason for his wakening. It is the call to a lifetime of work that is as transient and repetitive as the seasons. Only now, think of this artist leading others.

As a leader, Raymond inspires great loyalty and affection. His overwhelming desire to provide the very best hospitality to his guests, combined with an innate and powerful curiosity, an artist's eye for detail and the ability to analyse then create and implement long-term plans, make him an astute strategist, an attentive and demanding 'hands-on' manager, and a wonderful host. However, he battles continually to balance his idealistic nature with the realities of running a business. His example reminds everyone about the challenge and necessity of combining creativity with the financial practicality of leading a successful business, of the need for an idealist to have commercially focused advisors who also understand and are committed to his, or her, overarching vision.

As a young man Raymond was unsure what career to pursue. It took him time, he says, to 'find his passion'. He believes that everyone has a passion and that if it is not immediately obvious all one has to do is search for it. He is a man who believes in the power of emotion deliberately directed. It is, he argues, an essential requirement for success.

Not surprisingly then, Le Manoir aux Quat'Saisons is a business built on emotion that is presented through effective and efficient processes, and progressed through the application of corporate realistic creativity. It reflects who Raymond Blanc is and what he continues to learn. It reveals both the quality of his staff and his instinctive understanding of the need for an expert to be also an exemplary, lifelong student. It reinforces the relationship between progress and practicality, customer service and commercial reality, leadership and learning.

Raymond admits, 'Everything I do is led by an ideal that is never betrayed. But that ideal must correspond to a commercial side. That means the ideal runs separately and yet together with the commercial, but never the commercial first.' He goes on to explain, 'The ideal and the commercial necessity are opposites. They coexist together, but they repel each other very often. I learnt that many years ago because I was a raging idealist. I would only think of beauty and never the cost. I have done it, suffered from it, made my mistakes.'

The ideal that Raymond Blanc speaks of, that drives him, is so powerful that it appears to offer no choice. It has to be pursued, hunted down in the way that a starving man chases the promise of a potential meal. And yet the paradox is that this all-demanding ideal, this need to provide the very best hospitality, luxury and generosity to others, was given life by the man himself. It is the result of his imagination fuelled by a passion that is all-consuming. It has created a sense of drive within him that can sometimes leave others in its wake. Certainly, his desire to provide the very best for his guests has meant that, at times, his personal and family life have suffered. The cost of transforming and then establishing Le Manoir went far beyond finance, effort and time. His marriage ended as a consequence and his relationship with his sons was also damaged for a time. Raymond reflects, 'I realised, but only through hindsight, that a relationship needs as much love and care and nurturing as a beautiful dish, garden or hotel.'

Despite Raymond's acceptance of the need to agree to some compromises in the pursuit of his ideal, he still finds it a challenging process. He admits that, 'There is always an element of frustration. But life is all about learning. You learn that you cannot get what you cannot afford. You learn that there are all sorts of operational problems about creating a new project. You learn that you never get all the cash that you want. You learn that there are many reasons why something might not happen in the shape you first dreamt it. But I have learned to compromise... Now I think that compromise is not like a nasty disease. We all compromise in all of our lives, for example life throws at you the unexpected, things you cannot control, and to succeed sometimes you have to compromise. It is natural. I feel really happy that, over the years, I have never betrayed my core values. And I have compromised – but never to the point where I would sell out. To learn this was the biggest fight of my life, the hardest thing to do.'

The clash between Raymond's desire to create beauty and luxury and the financial realities of running a successful business is well demonstrated through his involvement in the design and styling of the house and rooms. 'I am,' he says, 'very much involved in the design of the place. For example, some years ago I travelled to Southeast Asia and I saw a mountain. It was terraced. It was incredible and beautiful, and immediately I saw in my mind a bedroom, a perfect bedroom, one that had never been imagined before by any designer, and I put my mind on that bedroom. We had a room in which we could do a refurbishment, a fifteen-metre space we could turn into a twenty-metre space. We could create steps leading up to the bed with a beautiful balustrade so that the bed is effectively one metre above the rest of the room, and then I've got my mountain! So imagine coming into a room with a flat ceiling at first and then you see this dramatic view of this beautiful bed, set as if it is on a pedestal, like a snow queen, and then – then! – you can open the roof and there are aquariums which, at the touch of a button, you can bring down for the night. And everything in the room is handmade and the bathroom is a pleasure dome!'

And so, working closely with professional designer Emily Todhunter, Raymond designed the room and then, 'I presented my proposal to the board, explaining that it was going to cost half a million pounds. I could prove to them, mind you, that I could pay it back in two years. The board loved the idea, but thought it was a big risk to take and they said "No". At first you feel... well, you want perfection and now you are like the little boy who wants his toy and can't play anymore. So you have to go away and come back with something positive, a scaled-down version that will be acceptable to everyone and still be extremely beautiful. Which is what I did, and that room is now one of the four bestsellers in the House! So everything is led by an ideal, that is the creative side.'

This ability to manage idealism, creativity and commercial necessity is crucial to Le Manoir's success and continuing appeal. Raymond is astute in the selection of his senior managers. Many have been with him for years. Some have left only to return. He refers to them as his 'field marshals', because not only do they understand and share his vision, they play a critical role in implementing it.

Raymond Blanc demonstrates an acute awareness of his own characteristics and tendencies. He talks about his weaknesses and mistakes as easily as he does his successes and passion. His 'field marshals' are charged with orchestrating the grand strategic plan and with providing a degree of balance, an alternative perspective, when their leader's idealism is in danger of overshadowing business necessities. By his own admission, though, Raymond remains the ultimate decision-maker. 'There is a slight autocratic side to it, because sometimes when I feel really strongly about something I do it. But I will always listen. I will always bring my team together and ask...'

At the head of that team is Philip Newman-Hall, the highly respected Director and General Manager of Le Manoir aux Quat'Saisons. He is a man who is clear about the essential difference between those who lead and those who only manage. In an interview for the *Fine Dining Guide* he explained it thus: 'Leaders and managers are perhaps two different characters with different skill sets. A leader has the vision and managers put the vision into practice. A leader will be charismatic, sell and follow up on their vision, communicate well with all levels of people. A leader, too, will be seen from the front and give and receive respect.'

This distinction is highlighted by the relationship Philip shares with Raymond and the different roles they play in the continuation and development of Le Manoir. Philip explains, 'I see Raymond as the leader. He has the vision and the ideas. I channel them into practical realities and lead the team behind me at that point. Essentially I cascade down RB's ethos and how we look after people both in the present and for the future. I'm the facilitator. My role is to make certain that we never stop the process. No matter what happens, no matter how difficult situations might be, we have to ensure that we never stop training people.'

Philip's respect and admiration for Raymond is reciprocated enthusiastically. When Philip won the 'Manager of the Year' award at the *Caterer and Hotelkeeper*'s annual hospitality awards held at Grosvenor House in London in 2011, Raymond

Blanc was quick to acknowledge, 'Philip and I have always worked closely together on each project. He understands the vision that drives Le Manoir and is able to help realise these dreams. These qualities make him a brilliant hotelier and a unique general manager. I am extremely proud to have him leading my team and look forward to working with him for many years to come.'

Interestingly, the panel, whilst voting unanimously to name Philip as the recipient of the award,[2] noted specifically his ability to command the admiration and respect of his boss!

Whilst the boss is a proud and passionate Frenchman, Philip Newman-Hall has about him a style and manner that is quintessentially English. He presents a mixture of the highest levels of professionalism. He has the ability to combine the welcome of the genial host with the quiet reserve and sense of duty of the ship's captain, and hiding behind this, one suspects, is a mischievous, boyish sense of humour coupled with a quietly independent spirit and a willingness to play.

At work, Philip projects a sense of calm certainty and authority. His enthusiasm for both the place and his role within it, is controlled and revealed in deliberate measure. When he says, 'If you have a passion for something you just love doing it every day, and it does still give me a buzz every day,' he speaks in a carefully modulated tone that is so different from the way his leader expresses himself and yet is just as compelling. And when he talks of his colleagues, those who are relatively new to the industry and those who are acknowledged as leaders in their own right, he gives an insight into why he is the General Manager here, why he is so highly regarded within Le Manoir and beyond. 'I've been in the industry for forty years now and I'm still reinventing my skills. The fact that I'm working with such talented and aspirational people drives me every day. It's not a competition – and yet it is! In a way, I have to be better than them every day.'

---

2   In the same awards ceremony Le Manoir won the 'Hotel of the Year – Group' award.

Within moments of first making his acquaintance one gets the sense that this is a man driven by attention to detail and the highest of standards. It is easy to imagine that he is very good at staying calm under pressure and that he is more than willing to trust his own judgement. His is a continual presence throughout Le Manoir. His approach as a manager is to see and be seen. It is an approach he adopted when he first joined The House in 1999. He stayed for five years, left to work as a consultant and then in 2009 received a phone call from Raymond asking him to consider returning. 'I wasn't expecting it, but I didn't have to think about it,' Philip says. 'It felt like the right time to come back. The question at Le Manoir is always, "What's the next project?" There's constant enthusiasm and revival.'

This enthusiasm, Philip acknowledges, stems from a primary source. 'It is due to the passion, vision and commitment of Raymond Blanc that Le Manoir is effectively reinventing itself every five years. So everything is, in a way, always new and exciting.'

What does remain constant, other than Raymond's perpetual drive for perfection, are the many senior staff who stay to share in the repeated reinventions. When Philip returned in 2009, twenty-two of the twenty-six senior team members were still present. One of these was Benoît Blin, who has been the Chef Pâtissier at Le Manoir since 1995. Under his leadership the pastry team has grown from five to thirteen in number, making it bigger than some entire kitchen brigades.

In an interview with *The Staff Canteen* Benoît said, 'When I joined Monsieur Blanc here, obviously he had a dream, and he was making his dream work; he had the establishment, and the person I found in Monsieur Blanc in 1995 was somebody really, really honourable... When I arrived I set a three-month goal, and perhaps I'd take my suitcase and go again, because we didn't know the future. You know, because when you don't know somebody, you listen to them and you see how much is true, how much does that person believe in what he says, and luckily for me I discovered he means every single word he says... The main difference with this establishment and many other establishments is it never stands still. And that's why I've stayed, because I could've stayed two years that's it, I've done it, it's time to go; but Le Manoir always moves up and up, even still now, it still moves on every day.'

It is this approach instigated by Raymond and supported by his senior staff that, according to Philip, ensures 'the balance of consistency' throughout the ongoing journey for improvement and the inevitable challenge of creating the most appropriate compromise between idealism and commercial reality.

iii) Learning and the Beauty of Ownership

Raymond Blanc has been at the forefront of many changes within the industry. On occasion he has been a lone voice championing a cause, although he denies that he is at all brave. All that is required to stand alone, he argues, is instinct and passion. When these two combine courage is not needed. What is necessary, though, is the willingness to keep learning.

The man who said that 'life is about learning' has used this philosophy to create an exemplary learning organisation based on the twin values of ongoing professional and personal development and the acceptance of ownership. Simply put, at Le Manoir managers are required to take responsibility for the overall performance of their team and for the behaviours of team members, and beyond that every individual is expected to assume responsibility for the quality of their delivery and the outputs they create.

Gary Jones, who has been the Executive Head Chef at The House for All Seasons since 1999, explains both the nature of, and the need for, ownership by way of a silent nod towards the inevitability of human imperfection. He says, 'I own every mistake made in my kitchen, even if it happens on my day off. It is my responsibility to re-train staff or to remind them of the need for standards. Every consistent end product needs productive, effective and efficient systems in place to produce it. This is as true for the purchasing of the raw ingredients as it is for the finished dish. We not only put requirements on our staff, we also do on our suppliers.

'For example, the guy on the back door looking at the fresh deliveries coming in to us every day is one of my senior chefs. He feels responsibility for what produce comes into my kitchen. When he is assessing the quality of the deliveries he must be certain before accepting anything. If there is any doubt in his mind, he must call me over.

'You see, systems create accountability and make people realise their part within the structure of things. Ultimately, systems are created by deciding what is best for the guests, for your team, for consistency. So, for us, if there is any problem with any aspect of a dish, we can trace it back to a specific individual within the kitchen team. I can then ask them to taste the dish, ask them questions about it and encourage them to tell me what is wrong with it. That way I learn more about them. You've got to listen if you want to know how best to develop your staff. And it's essential that we do provide training and support constantly because, you know, when you add human beings to any system...'

Le Manoir aux Quat'Saisons employs over two hundred and thirty human beings all of whom benefit from a detailed and rigorous induction programme and ongoing training opportunities. No matter how much Raymond Blanc might trust and value his own instinct and passion, he leaves nothing to chance when it comes to ensuring that his staff understand his philosophy and can put it into practice.

New staff undertake an induction programme lasting up to eight weeks. It begins with an introduction to the house, meeting first with key personnel and then with Raymond himself, who provides an explanation of his vision and the aims of the business. After this, everyone enjoys dinner in the restaurant to ensure they understand fully the guests' experience. They also receive a Welcome Pack, a simple booklet that includes an initial greeting and message from their team leader, introductions to each member of the team with their photos included, and an array of practical information. Irrespective of which team the new member of staff is joining, every Welcome Pack has one common page, titled 'Our Philosophy, Our Aim', written by

Raymond Blanc. The page begins:

'**Excellence** is an accumulation of seemingly meaningless details we build from love, intelligence, patience and teamwork. Eventually one has volume and density. One is reaching excellence; one is touching the sublime. **The good does not interest us but the sublime does.**

'Our aim at Le Manoir is to create a centre of excellence in all of its many facets i.e. garden, reception, maintenance, welcome, food, rooms...

'Each of these facets is part... of overall success. So each of us, regardless of the levels of our responsibilities, have **ownership** in the **success** of reaching our **goals**.'

During their first months in employment, every new member of staff spends some days working in each department, including the kitchens, to further their appreciation of what everyone does and how they all connect.

Before induction, though, applicants experience a recruitment process designed to ensure that those who are employed possess the personality traits, beliefs and values that match the culture and aspirations of the business. It is a process led by Le Manoir's HR manager Julia Murrell, who has implemented both short- and long-term recruitment strategies. She explains, 'One of my key goals was to implement low-cost or no-cost recruitment methods. We developed short-term, internet-based strategies, getting us out into national and European associations, using our relationships with these to attract people who would want to work here. This is vital, because people who come to work here have to want to work here. Our website was changed to include more job-based advertising. Also our work with schools, colleges and universities is part of our long-term recruitment strategy. In 2010 only 2% of our recruitment was from our existing talent bank – people we knew or who had worked here before. In 2011 over 21% was from our talent bank and we are looking to double this. We created five positions for internships in the restaurant team.

And, incredibly, we have internships now in all departments – including housekeeping!'

Julia argues that the ability to encourage applications from the best possible individuals is dependent on a mixture of networking, analysis and, importantly, creative thinking. 'In these times you have to attract the right people,' she says. 'To do this you have to think outside the box. We are always outward-facing.' However, in her HR role Julia is, of course, always internally-facing, too. One of her first priorities was to develop an understanding, and gain the trust, of her peers. 'The other managers here made it very easy and welcoming for me when I started,' she recalls. 'They do really encourage you to form a relationship with them. They let me do whatever I wanted to in the first six months.' And Julia's innovations proved to be so successful that, 'Now I shortlist for every department. We (HR) spend time with each manager. We determine what type of person they are looking for. Our focus now is on behavioural recruitment training. We do everything necessary to identify the best applicants. We want to know what makes a person tick. We want to know about their personality – how adaptable and flexible they are.'

Julia's own recruitment experience when joining Le Manoir was equally rigorous, if less formal in nature. 'I was interviewed by both Philip and RB,' she says. 'Philip had a very clear idea about what he wanted from me. When I met Philip I was immediately engaged by him, he really is a people manager. Then I met RB. He spent two hours with me. He wanted to know how I went about doing things.' Once employed, though, Julia was to do more than simply introduce examples of best practice from her previous organisational experience. 'Le Manoir is unique and the challenges it presents demand bespoke solutions. It quickly became obvious to me that I had to create and implement specific HR policies and strategies – different from anything I had created before.'

The philosophy of human resource management that Julia has developed is based on, 'Treating the staff as guests. If we are seeking to provide five-star service to our guests, we need to provide the same level of service to our staff. It is about seeing each member of staff as an individual investment. Everyone's HR plan has their name, not their role, on it. Things are done as much as possible on an individual basis. If a member of staff walks into the HR office we stop whatever we are doing and address them fully. We tend to adopt the approach of saying "Yes" and then working out how to do it. For example, one of our porters said that he had always wanted to do a sign-language course. So we signed him on one! And now, if ever one of our guests needs to speak in sign language, we have someone who can. The bottom line is that even a support department like HR has to have a guest focus.'

The principle of treating the staff as guests is demonstrated in two ways: through the provision of ongoing professional training and through practical, personal welfare and wellbeing support. Julia explains, 'This is a demanding industry, particularly at our level. Beyond that, there are things that happen in people's lives that they don't want their HR manager, or any other manager, to know about. So we launched an Employee Assistance helpline in January 2012. It's a free telephone number that allows our staff to speak to someone who can help with all issues – stress, childcare, relationship problems and so on. We also recommend exercise to our staff, ensure they are properly hydrated during the day and have fresh fruit available.'

To say that there are opportunities for staff training and professional development at Le Manoir would be like saying that cars race at Silverstone. The two go hand in hand. In the words of Philip Newman-Hall, 'We are a training academy, a centre of learning for the industry. We have a generosity of learning. As an organisation we have to match RB's personal generosity. I have to ensure that this philosophy pervades every department. It's not all about money. We see this as an investment for the future, not a cost. It's sometimes hard to talk to accountants about how much money we spend on this sort of thing. However, it is essential for the continued success of Le Manoir. The day we stop doing this we will go downhill.'

Benoît Blin emphasises the necessity of training and continual learning and compares it to his own experiences. 'Within their first six months we make sure that staff have got an up-to-date health and safety, food hygiene, and all the basic training necessary,' he says. 'It's compulsory. It's part of our commitment to the industry and to our chefs, but this is where it starts. From there you will learn to manage and develop your skills. We are sending you onto courses, we are sending you off after two years with us, in France amongst the MOF[3] of France in specialised schools, all paid for. In my day, it was the opposite. I had to pay for every single one of them, I had to create the time. Here, the effort is already made for you.' And Benoît admits that making the effort for those in his team, through daily mentoring and the provision of training opportunities, 'Is the most rewarding thing I do.'

For Philip, there is a sense of obligation, an ethical requirement, to develop the industry stars of the future. 'I'm only trying to put back into the industry what people gave to me when I started,' he says. 'I think you have a moral responsibility to put back.' He does this by also playing his part in supporting a range of industry-relevant academic partnerships, including the 'Adopt a School' scheme.

At Le Manoir, however, much of this 'putting back' is done during the day-to-day work of all involved. Philip is quick to point out that, 'So much of our development is done on the job, not just through formal training.' And Gary Jones reinforces both this point and the significance of the learning and training culture when he says, 'I don't just want me to have this skill. I want everyone around me to have it. Again, that's where systems come in. The detail that goes into one dish, like a risotto, the micro-attention to detail throughout is so important. I need every guy in my section to be able to produce and that takes time, training and patience. It's like raising your kids, it isn't going to happen overnight and they have to feel that constant

---

3   The title of *Un des Meilleurs Ouvriers de France* is earned in a competition held every four years to determine the Best Craftsmen of France.

care. A recipe won't teach people how to produce a great dish. You have to touch the person, look them in the eye, train them.' All staff are encouraged to learn from their occasional errors and from feedback received. If mistakes occur, members of staff take personal responsibility and the lessons are then learned and shared. Junior members of staff are encouraged to question their leaders. The principle that 'everyone can learn from everyone else' is well established. Feedback is the lifeblood of the organisation; it isn't just welcomed: it is hunted. Mourad Ben Tefka, the Restaurant Manager, confirms with a slight smile, 'Feedback is the breakfast of champions.' He goes on, 'I ask my team to face all situations and I would not hesitate to say "This is an error you have made and now we have to find out why and then we can learn as a team or even as a company."'

It is common practice, too, for staff to take part in a range of culinary, management and service-related competitions, both nationally and internationally. They invariably place highly. Successes are publicised and celebrated. When Benoît was asked to become the President of the UK Pastry team for the 2011 Coupe du Monde de la Pâtisserie held in Lyon, France, it became another significant opportunity for a mixture of challenge, sharing and promotion. With only a few months in which to prepare and motivate the team and with the UK having very limited experience in the competition, Benoît set the demanding target of a top-ten finish. Incredibly, the team finished ninth. 'I was so proud to represent our industry and so we needed to create our own, small thing,' Benoît says with a smile and an unconscious straightening of his back. 'We picked two candidates for the team, one of whom was from Le Manoir. We are doing this for goodwill more than anything at the moment, but now we have to get sponsorship. We want youngsters from Britain to enter this every two years and to promote the pastry industry which is currently under-promoted. Ours is a skill that, if not promoted, will disappear.'

The philosophy behind entering competitions is simple: passionate people are keen to develop their passion further, so they need to be supported, trained and challenged; as they improve so does the service and experience they offer to guests.

Inevitably some staff will move on, taking the skills and attitudes they have developed at Le Manoir with them. The number of highly skilled chefs and managers working within the industry who have spent time learning and developing their craft under the leadership of Raymond Blanc is significant. Philip Newman-Hall reflects, 'The House has spawned many successful people and we tend to keep in touch. Raymond is a giving person and people tend to give it back to him. There must be approaching twenty chefs who have gone through the kitchens here and gone on to Michelin stardom in their own right. It's not just about the chefs either: Le Manoir has seen, for example, an international community of future successful Hotel General Managers who have enjoyed their time at the property and also tend to stay in touch.'

The value of learning and the beauty of ownership lie in the fact that they are at once personal and social, incorporating transmission and sharing, ensuring individual, organisational and, eventually, industry development. Raymond Blanc once wrote for his staff, 'Le Manoir is a school of thoughts and we must remain leaders in our industry.' This mixture of learning and leading also plays an important part in the organisation's strategic planning and marketing, as Raymond's story about duvets and blankets demonstrates.

iv) Duvets and Blankets

Just as learning and ownership work hand in hand at Le Manoir so, too, do curiosity and strategic development. Raymond Blanc and his senior team seek to understand fully the needs of current and future guests. It is this understanding that drives staff training and changes in strategy. Sometimes an insight gained into one very specific aspect of the business can lead to a strategic shift. RB explains:

'I asked two hundred of our guests, "Do you prefer duvets or blankets?" On the face of it, it seems a very silly question. However, I got a very fascinating answer. Sixty per cent of our guests preferred duvets and forty per cent preferred blankets. So I asked them a second question. It was, "How strongly do you feel about duvets and how strongly do you feel about blankets?" It was an amazing answer! Ninety per cent felt very strongly about duvets and ninety per cent felt very strongly about blankets. I then asked them, "Why do you feel so strongly?" Because to me a blanket is luxury, it is so nurturing, it makes me feel all tucked in. And a duvet is about freedom, modernity, about rolling around with no boundaries. How does this translate into business? I think that if as a business you can, in one fell swoop, undermine sixty per cent of your customers, or forty per cent of them, then you are in trouble. And just by simply offering blankets we are undermining so many of our guests. So that is not good business.

'For me, luxury today is very different from what it was yesterday. Yesterday luxury was about gold taps and heavy carpets and chintz everywhere, and waiters looking very important, telling you what to eat and so on. In the last ten or maybe even six years luxury has changed. The modern guest is often exhausted. They have little or no time for themselves or even their family. So when our guests come here we have to create a relaxing environment, one that nurtures them and their family, which opens its arms to them and gives them the best moment of their lives.

'So, when I discovered this about the bed linen I immediately said that we should now think very differently. When I first said that we should change our thinking about bed linen I was asked, "What about storage? What about cost? What about training?" I understood that. However, I said, "Let's find the space and the money and provide the training." Because when you are one hundred per cent sure, you know…

'Because of that information about duvets and blankets we asked more questions of our guests. And because of their answers we changed everything. We changed the menus. We moved Le Manoir to a quiet modernity, to the 21st century, but without following cheap fashion, because this place is never led by fashion.'

Actually, that simple question about duvets and blankets was the springboard that led to a new five-year strategic plan. Raymond's innate curiosity and desire to predict and then shape the future is a quality more usually looked for in a politician than a chef. The sense he gives, though, is that he cannot help himself. 'I spend so much time trying to understand our guests,' he admits. 'And what is the biggest change going to be in five or ten years' time? Nutrition. There's no doubt about it. We are going to eat far better than we do now. And that means gastronomy will have to change. That means the offering, the way it is served, and what is being served... So that is what I do, I try to steer this place towards the truly important changes in the lifestyle of our guests.'

The place is steered through daily operations that are well planned and practised, disciplined and, at times, seemingly militaristic in nature. Heads of Department meet regularly. There are briefings before each restaurant service. The gardening team is kept informed of all events to ensure that their day-to-day work never damages the guests' experience. Gardening work never starts early, for example, near those bedrooms in which guests might be expected to sleep late.

This focus on ongoing strategic planning and daily attention to detail springs from the desire to provide ever-better service to guests, rather than a competitive need to out-perform other hotels and restaurants. Indeed, according to Philip Newman-Hall, 'Our competition is not another country house hotel, it is another quite expensive, aspirational experience. For example, a weekend in Paris, or a helicopter ride.'

And so, in a world filled with a wide variety of such aspirational opportunities, marketing plays a significant role in bringing the message of Le Manoir to public attention, and keeping it there. The explicit marketing strategy is based on creating media stories and appropriate business partnerships. The implicit strategy grows out of the learning culture that permeates the place. Philip Newman-Hall makes the point that, 'Our learning culture is as important a marketing tool as the guest experience.'

The business that regards itself as a training academy for the industry understands that its own reputation is reinforced and enhanced by the quality and capability of the staff who leave to work elsewhere. Philip says, 'We have to accept that people will move on. The day they know it is right to leave, we should help them with that transition, training them up if necessary before they go, and then keeping in touch with them.'

Gary Jones, a man who, by his own admission, has had to learn how to mentor and train staff, offered an example of that approach in practice. 'One of my guys is moving on after six years with me. I've talked to him, making his future prospects clear. I've advised him where to go and work next. At this point in his career it is right for him to go away, gain some different experiences, and then realise that there is no place like home. RB just wants to give everything he's got. He wants everyone to succeed, develop and grow. He wants us to pass it on.'

By passing it on Gary and the other senior managers send out professional ambassadors who, by adding value throughout the industry, ensure that the status of Le Manoir aux Quat'Saisons remains centre stage, and that it attracts like-minded individuals who want to work at the highest level and who want to learn.

Not surprisingly, Raymond Blanc is at the heart of all the implicit and explicit marketing. He is the figurehead. His television work and the many interviews he gives are central to the promotion of The House. He understands fully how to share the brand values and he is as accomplished at doing it through the media as he is through the design of Le Manoir itself – where even something as simple as a lavender path has its own, significant part to play.

v) The Lavender Path

Upon leaving their cars, guests walk towards the House along a lavender path. Lavender is synonymous with Provence. For guests who have been there it is intended to remind them of that time. For those who have not visited or do not know the connection, the path is both attractive to look at and wonderful to smell. It is beautiful, cost-effective and functional. It is another indication of how Raymond Blanc always combines his clear sense of personal and professional identity with a desire for beauty and, in this instance, shrewd business acumen.

He explains, 'When you think about lavender, first it is beautiful. I have chosen a particular variety that flowers for three months and is resistant to anything the British weather will throw at it and, equally, it needs very little maintenance. So that very simplicity, a lavender path, which is one micro-element of what we do here, at first it is beautiful, first it is French, first it reaffirms the brand and makes people smile. Everything is very much taken on these values.'

The House, like the gardens, reflects the life, interests and personality of its creator. Here tradition plays host to originality, cultures mix, comfort combines with sensuality. Most guests are either regulars or people visiting to celebrate a special occasion. The responsibility to live up to guests' expectations by ensuring a memorable occasion is taken very seriously by all. Both Raymond Blanc and Philip Newman-Hall believe that this can only be achieved if staff understand the entirety of the guests' experience.

Philip says, 'As a point of departure, put yourself in the place of the guest and think of how you would like to be treated. Think about the standard and the level of service that you would expect and deliver against those expectations.' Philip ensures that he sleeps in every bedroom twice a year, entering into the experience as much as he possibly can from the guest's perspective. All the staff are also encouraged to become guests once a year. This serves not only as a form of reward, but also to remind them of what it feels like to be a guest at Le Manoir. Philip explains, 'We offer our staff the chance to dine with us at a significantly reduced rate, bringing family or friends with them, so that they see things through the guests' eyes.'

The restaurant (and therefore, by extension, the kitchen) is, according to Philip, the heart of the House. The three people charged with keeping this particular heart healthy are Gary Jones, Benoît Blin and Mourad Ben Tefka. Gary Jones's philosophy about cooking and the sharing of food is rich with emotion. 'I delight in taking raw ingredients and creating pleasure. The joy you can give by providing a meal is so great. Food is the biggest subject on the planet, whether it's diet, health, sharing, or just pure enjoyment. Through my cooking I want to touch people's hearts and souls. Food is more than fuel. It lifts people's spirits. Food is a gift. It can become a joyous, emotional memory. On some level food always makes us think, and feel, of home. That's why food will never go out of fashion.'

Benoît's personal motivation has never changed. 'I would say it's the same as the one to begin, which is, you don't look at what you do today, you look at what you want to do tomorrow. So the motivation today is still the same, which is going beyond what you are capable of, training yourself beyond what you know.'

Benoît's experiences at Le Manoir have helped him to develop as a manager and mentor, not just as a chef. 'When I first managed a team I didn't do very well at the beginning,' he confesses. 'The mentality in France was "You are the best at what you do, so teach others!" At the age of 21 I was Chef de Partie in the Ritz in Paris, but my management style and skills were rubbish! I had no understanding of what management means. One of the things I've learned here through our internal training is knowing who I am. I am quite fiery by nature. Sometimes I have to say to myself "My frustration is mine, not the other person's." So I will remove myself until I am in a better state of mind.

'Le Manoir has helped me to move from being a good chef to a still-learning manager. Now I am using all of my experience to make sure that people in my team don't make the mistakes I did. Three of them have done competitions. When they come back I tell them to coach the others. I am only one mind and we are stronger together, sharing ideas.'

In the restaurant Mourad and his team of more than forty staff provide the service and create the atmosphere designed to match the quality of Gary and Benoît's cooking. Menus include a five-, six-, seven- and nine-course option, and an à la carte and vegetarian selection. Before any new dish can be placed on a menu it has to meet with Raymond's approval. The front of house team is calm and attentive, disguising their concentration and focus whilst walking with well-practised ease the fine line between friendliness and professional courtesy. Here, Mourad is a softly-spoken director of operations who quietly observes, monitors and controls the beat, the pulse, at the very core of The House. He likens restaurant service to theatre, a form of performance, although he is quick to acknowledge that, 'You have to give a different performance every day.'

Whilst Mourad appreciates the need for effective and efficient organisational routines, he is also aware that a sense of repetition brings with it the danger of complacency. Even here, in a business that is open every day, the show must go on each time as if it is for the first and last time. 'Anything can become routine,' Mourad says. 'So I tell my team that we need to challenge each other, all of us, at every level. By challenging each other every day we can overcome complacency. We have to remember always that we are here for our guests. For example, someone may have saved for years to come here and this is our one chance to shine in front of them.'

Le Manoir aux Quat'Saisons offers more than just fine dining and luxurious accommodation, however. Throughout the year there are also a variety of events. These include musical evenings and carol services at Christmas in the local church. And there is a well-established cookery school offering one-, two- or four-day courses for everyone from children to adults, from complete beginners to experienced enthusiasts.

Whatever the guests' reason for visiting, and whatever the season, Le Manoir aux Quat'Saisons reminds all that with sufficient passion, vision and continual learning, dreams can be turned into positive and enduring business realities. Ultimately, The House for All Seasons works with nature to encourage people to celebrate the most important things in life.

vi) The Football Fan in the Church

In one important sense this is a story of one man's search and of the ways he has sought out, attracted and motivated the most appropriate individuals to join him. At its core it is a search for connection, for a connection with nature, with the soil and all it can produce; for a connection between cultures; for a connection with an ideal that inspires passion and which, tantalisingly and appropriately, can never be truly reached; for a connection with people in the sharing of food and meaningful experiences, in the creation of memories, in the development of an industry.

When Raymond Blanc found his passion he used the energy and the drive that gave him to create a vibrant, challenging and clear vision and then dedicated his life to making it a reality. To do this, of course, he had to share it with others. The result is Le Manoir aux Quat'Saisons.

Raymond's example highlights the power of a detailed vision and shows how such a vision grows out of and, in turn, fuels an emotionally compelling sense of purpose. A dynamic, passionate and charismatic leader, Raymond Blanc combines emotional compulsion with strategic acuity; an autocratic tendency with a willingness to delegate and be influenced by others; an artist's flair and a general's determination. He demonstrates and shares an energy that challenges, motivates and inspires. He expects only the very best from himself and his staff. The man they call 'RB' does not simply 'walk the talk', he sprints it. And he has maintained that pace for decades. Whilst charisma is a quality that cannot be taught, many of his other attributes can.

The story of Le Manoir demonstrates the need for leaders to set an inspirational example, to be congruent in their words and behaviours, to create emotional support for both themselves and their vision and, importantly, to surround themselves with trusted, capable and like-minded individuals who act on their behalf. Raymond's 'field marshals' understand not only what he is seeking to achieve but also, importantly, how he wants to achieve it. The 'field marshals' put Raymond's plans into action; they are the ones with whom he is most likely to share his thoughts. They are also individuals who, no matter what their own level of experience and expertise, are comfortable maintaining a relatively low public profile whilst their leader performs the role of figurehead in the way that only he can.

Within Le Manoir Raymond Blanc has created a learning organisation built on a culture that emphasises ownership and personal responsibility. The high standards he sets place everlasting demands on his staff and these, coupled with his instinctive desire to share, encourage and empower, have led inevitably to the development of a centre of learning that benefits guests, staff and the industry at large. The relationship between learning and ownership cannot be overstated. The process of learning requires all parties involved – those who are learning and those who are teaching – to take responsibility for both the quality of the interaction and the quality of the outcome. What is equally true is that a mistake, an unintended and undesirable outcome, can only become a truly powerful source of learning once an individual or team takes ownership of it.

To create a learning organisation is to acknowledge that everyone involved, irrespective of status or expertise, can develop their knowledge and performance; it is to place a premium value on feedback and the necessity of acting creatively and appropriately on that; it is to put purpose above ego, to run desire through systems and structures, to balance wanting more tomorrow with an appreciation of today. At its heart, it requires that you know precisely who you are and that you can always become a better version of yourself.

The apparent paradox is that Le Manoir's constant, clear and powerful sense of corporate identity is underpinned by a culture that encourages and enables change. Upon inspection, though, the paradox dissolves: the opportunities for individual learning and ongoing organisational reinvention happen *around* the essential essence of the place. The message from The House for All Seasons is that identity is created and maintained by an unswerving vision and purpose that are, for their part, dependent upon the lifeblood of learning.

The message is also that recruitment, selection and induction processes play a crucial role in the maintenance and sharing of 'who you are'. Here the emphasis is on attracting people who fit the established culture, rather than always prioritising experience and skill. After all, a learning organisation can develop individual capability. Passion, on the other hand, cannot be taught. It has to be found. By requiring every member of staff to work in every department, the senior managers at Le Manoir ensure that everyone appreciates the totality of the business; by encouraging them to revisit as guests, they mix reward with a clear reminder of their raison d'être.

Once, on a winter evening, Le Manoir hosted a musical event and dinner with the great tenor Russell Watson. He sang to a small audience in the nearby church before all retired to the House for a five-course meal. That afternoon Russell Watson was rehearsing in the church dressed in his favourite Manchester United football kit. To hear his voice coming out of the building as he sang an 'Ave Maria' was both beautiful and appropriate. To see him rehearsing dressed as a footballer was a reminder that even exceptionally talented people are in many ways just the same as the people they entertain, serve or lead. Russell Watson is one of the world's greatest tenors and is also a football fan like millions of others. The individuals who create, manage and develop such businesses as Le Manoir aux Quat'Saisons are ordinary people, too. They do extraordinary things because they have found their passion. Through their commitment to excellence, they come to know who they are, and they share that with us in ways that are both congruent and inspirational.

3

The World at the End of the Road: The Waterside Inn, Bray

'Serving is pleasing'

Diego Masciaga

Introduction

This is a story about a dynasty and an institution and about what it takes to stay at the top of your profession for a quarter of a century. It is a story about innovation leading to tradition and a sense of establishment. It is a story about the creation, management and sharing of power and of the loneliness of leadership. It is about the pressure of living up to a great reputation and, most importantly, of knowing how to follow a revolution with evolution. It is a story that asks if, ultimately, anything really changes at all.

The story of The Waterside Inn offers lessons about:
- The nature of change and methods of change management
- The power of organisational culture
- The creation, management and sharing of power
- The loneliness of leadership
- The prices you risk paying for achieving and maintaining excellence.

It is a story that begins with one man.

i) The Patriarch

It is 9.50am on a bright Wednesday morning in August. Inside The Waterside Inn breakfast is being served to the residents. Outside the River Thames sparkles slightly in the early morning sun. Diego Masciaga has just arrived. He has chosen to enter the building today through the kitchen. As Diego moves through the room he shares a greeting with Alain Roux. The chef/patron smiles briefly. The two men understand each other well.

Diego continues on his way, walking past his office and into the small reception area. Staff smile and nod respectfully when they see him. He speaks to them all. As Diego pauses in reception, running his finger along the underside of a coffee table, checking for dust, he glances inevitably at the photos on the wall. They show the Roux dynasty and his boss, Michel Roux Snr, the man he has worked for since 1973, the Patriarch of The Waterside Inn.

Nearly six hundred miles away, on the balcony of a chalet in Crans-Montana, Switzerland, the man Diego Masciaga refers to as 'Mr Michel' or 'Mr Roux' is taking a moment to enjoy the mountain view and the freshest of air. Michel Roux Snr is able to enjoy many such moments at his home in Switzerland. It is one of the main reasons he moved here.

'I love the walking, to listen to the cowbells in the peacefulness, to smell the fresh air, to eat the wild raspberries and blueberries, and to drink the mountain water. I feel so close to the sky here. We forget as we grow up to respect nature. But this is the closest to heaven you can get.'

Michel, one of the fathers of British gastronomy, has travelled full circle. Life in this part of Switzerland reminds him of what he knew as a child. For most of his adult life he has been a dominating force in the culinary world. The Waterside Inn, which he bought in 1972, became his second three-Michelin-starred restaurant. As one of the world's great chefs, he is used to being in control. At The Waterside Inn his power and influence are still evident and, when not in Switzerland, he spends much of his time travelling around the world as an ambassador for the restaurant. Here, though, in Crans-Montana, he enjoys the simplicity of having neighbours who are good friends, of being able to 'call on good people to have lunch or go for a walk.'

He also enjoys what he regards as an appropriate lack of political interference. 'Here Big Brother is not watching you, telling you what to do and what not to do, aspects of life that are now evident in France and the UK.'

Michel Roux Snr is a man of slight build with grey hair and a deep, at times almost lyrical, voice that carries the notes of authority, charm and humour with unconscious ease. He has a presence shared only by those individuals who are used to being in control. There is about him an unmistakable sense of accomplishment and personal drive, of a man who knows precisely what it takes to be outstanding in any profession and who is fully aware that he has achieved at the highest levels. He combines charisma with the power of the expert and, running deep behind the sophistication and artistry of the Master Chef and restaurateur, is the quiet, independent confidence and bold spirit of a revolutionary and explorer. According to Alain, his father is a perfectionist. It is a description Michel is happy to accept and explain.

'I think perfection is about being able to be very simple in life, adhering to the rule of being yourself. What I am saying is don't try to do what you are not able to do, but do whatever you can do and be yourself at it… When people can just be themselves, they can do wonderful things.'

His has been a life of study, work and commitment that has enabled him to make many wonderful things seem uncommonly simple. In a poll of UK chefs carried out by *Caterer and Hotelkeeper* magazine in 2003 Michel and his elder brother, Albert, were voted the two most influential chefs in the country. Seven years later, in May 2010, Michel and Alain invited every Michelin-starred chef in the UK and Ireland to attend a special party celebrating The Waterside's twenty-fifth year with three Michelin stars. The vast majority accepted. It was an event that marked both the outstanding consistency of the restaurant and the special role that Michel has played in the development of British gastronomy.

Whilst the distinguished guests enjoyed miniature finger versions of some of The Waterside's most famous dishes, Derek Bulmer, head of Michelin Great Britain, addressed them all. He said, 'What could be a better example of consistency than a restaurant that's held three stars for twenty-five consecutive years? During that time The Waterside has proved to be a great training kitchen for literally hundreds of chefs that have gone on to great things themselves – many of them going on to win stars of their own. The Roux Scholarship has grown to become one of the most respected of its kind. Michel, you've put a lot back into the industry and you've done a lot to promote and encourage new talent.'

He was not the only one to share his thanks and admiration. The Waterside's most famous culinary neighbour, Heston Blumenthal, expressed his respect and appreciation in musical terms, saying, 'I describe the Roux brothers as the Beatles of British gastronomy. There was food before and food after the Roux brothers, but the quality of the food in this country is that much better because of what Michel and Albert have done.'

The party was just one celebration of a lifetime of achievements based, according to Michel himself, on 'about forty per cent talent and sixty per cent determination, discipline and hard work day after day.'

It is a life that began in April 1941, ten months after Germany's defeat of France in the Second World War. Michel was born in Charolles, Saône-et-Loire. When the war ended, the family moved to Paris and his father opened a charcuterie. By the time Michel was a teenager he had decided to become a pâtissier and in June 1956 he accepted a three-year contract at Camille Loyal's pâtisserie in Belleville in northern Paris. After this he joined his brother, Albert, working at the British Embassy. He stayed there until the end of April 1960 when, on the recommendation of Émile Rouault, he took a post as *commis* in the kitchen of Cécile de Rothschild. By the age of twenty-two, despite a brief spell in the military, Michel had become the youngest chef ever employed by the Rothschild family. It was an indication of the great things to come.

When Albert moved to London, Michel joined him and in 1967 they opened Le Gavroche in Lower Sloane Street. The expressed aim was to 'achieve a worldwide reputation for the quality of our cuisine and service'. Which is precisely what they achieved. Under their joint leadership Le Gavroche went on to become the first British restaurant to gain three Michelin stars. In 1972, with several other successful restaurants under their banner, the brothers bought a traditional English pub in the quiet Berkshire village of Bray.

Michel recalls, 'By 1972 we were ready for a fresh adventure. I was exhausted all the time, but I was also a little bored. We thought we would like to bring the Roux London touch to the country and started looking around in the Thames Valley for a suitable property... It was actually François Merlozzi, a co-director, who discovered The Waterside Inn in Bray. As soon as I saw it, with its 100-year-old willow tree and its wonderful river frontage, I knew it was the perfect place. It was a nice pub, but had a grotty dining room. After buying the lease from the tenant (the pub was actually owned by Whitbreads), we borrowed as much money as we could from the bank in order to revamp the entire place, particularly the dining room overlooking the river.'

And so the pub was transformed and The Waterside Inn was created. By 1974 the first Michelin star was achieved and the second followed in 1977. It took a further eight years of hard, consistent work before the much-coveted third star was awarded. Michel had flown to Sydney, Australia, to join his wife, Robyn, for their winter holiday. He was informed on his arrival that Derek Brown, then head of Michelin in Britain, wanted to speak to him. After several moments of nervous pacing Michel picked up the phone and made the call. Derek confirmed the good news. It was at once the greatest of rewards and the greatest of challenges.

Michel wrote of the experience, 'According to Robyn, my neck started to go red and a rash rose up my face as the conversation got under way. I became speechless... I was both overwhelmed by the honour and daunted by the new pressure that I knew this would put on me. Not only had I worked hard to earn it, I knew I would now have to keep working just as hard to keep it.'

One year later the brothers separated their business interests and Michel became the sole owner of The Waterside Inn. Whilst the restaurant has continued to maintain its three Michelin stars, its patriarch has gone on to acquire many other accolades. These include the *Meilleur Ouvrier de France*, or 'best French craftsman' award for pâtisserie, a title received in 1976 of which he is particularly proud, an honorary OBE received in 2002 and the Chevalier de la Légion d'Honneur awarded in 2004.

Although Michel's name is no longer above the entrance to The Waterside, his is a constant and demanding presence. The photographs on the wall and the selection of his books that are for sale remind everyone as they pass through reception of the role he has played and continues to play. He is not only one of the world's great chefs, he is also a successful businessman. He was a revolutionary and is now the protector of a dynasty. And, like all leaders seeking to ensure their legacy, he has chosen his right-hand men well.

ii) The Hero

Diego Masciaga has been in charge of service at The Waterside Inn since 1988. He is a well-dressed Italian in his late forties with silver grey hair and a round face that smiles easily. He speaks several languages fluently, has an eye for detail and accepts no compromises when it comes to maintaining standards. Every morning Diego arrives at work at around 9.30am. He likes to vary his entrance.

'Sometimes,' he says, 'I come in through the front door. Sometimes I come in from the back. My staff know this is not to catch them out, rather it helps me to keep a fresh perspective, to see if things are out of place. If you enter a building through the same door every day you become used to seeing things in a certain way, you can become lazy. I cannot afford that.'

Staff greet Diego with a respectful nod. To them he is always 'Mr Diego'. He is their boss. It is impossible for anyone to forget this. He can do their jobs as well as he can his own. He is responsible for all aspects of The Waterside Inn apart from the kitchen. Some nights after a busy evening service he is still in his office at 2am checking finances, balancing the books, preparing for tomorrow. He has an excellent understanding of wine and cheese and is acknowledged as one of the best carvers in Europe. His philosophy, that 'Service is pleasing' and that service begins and ends with a genuine smile, drives all staff attitudes and behaviours.

Frédéric Poulette, the assistant maître d'hôtel, reinforces the point, saying, 'The most important thing I have learnt from Mr Diego is to smile, to be happy. You have to be happy with what you are doing. If you want to achieve something and you are not happy you won't reach it, you will not be willing to give 100%.'

Diego's skill, coupled with his commitment to support and develop all within his team, has earned him international recognition. In June 2010, at a private lunch held at The Waterside, Diego was presented with the Grand Prix de L'Art de la Salle by the International Academy of Gastronomy. Previously only ever awarded to two individuals, it identifies him as one of the pre-eminent restaurant managers in the world. In 2012 he was honoured by his home country with the title of *Cavaliere*. Yes, it is easy for everyone to remember that he is their leader. He can also be their confidant and supporter.

'Keeping my staff motivated is the priority,' Diego explains. 'Even if they are a kitchen porter washing dishes or a cleaner; first thing in the morning I go to see everyone in the same way. And they know when I approach them they can ask me questions. Everyone will tell me their problems. You see many of them are young and on their own. Many of them are foreigners. They know I will help them.'

He protects them, too, on the very rare occasions that customers behave inappropriately. 'I can accept anything apart from a guest being rude to my staff. If there is a guest who has maybe had too much to drink, who is starting to be rude, then I will put my foot down. The staff know that and feel good about it. It is one of the important ways I make the team believe in me and trust me and follow me.'

Diego likens himself to the conductor of a great orchestra. He directs. He orchestrates. He gives power and permission to his staff to perform to the best of their ability. And they know that, despite his personal involvement during every service, he is watching them all. When he describes his role he keeps a gentle smile on his face and just a hint of steel in his eyes.

'During service everybody here is in tune. In an orchestra some people play violins, some play the cello, some the trombone and so on. They are like my waiters. Some serve the bread, some serve the wine, some the cheese. I don't have a stick like a maestro with an orchestra. I don't stand alone in the middle. Instead, I am floating around. I see things my staff cannot see, so I can give them direction.'

His directions are followed precisely. If they are not, a private conversation follows. 'Sometimes I have to tell people off, because when you are young you cannot always see the effects of what you are doing. Around the corner somewhere out of the way I will see them and explain to them. I never do this in front of the guests. I never shout. There is no need to use horrible language. If there is a complaint, I take the blame from the guest. If it is a constructive criticism I will talk quietly to that member of the team. If it isn't I say nothing.'

No matter what the intrinsic levels of staff motivation or their personal expertise, Diego's leadership is an irresistible motivating force. He acknowledges, though, that he in turn works for the Roux family. He believes that it is essential to remember who the boss is, to recognise the space that exists between employer and employee. It is within this space, he argues, that disagreements can occur safely.

'With Mr Michel I always say Mr Roux. I've been with him for twenty-eight years, but I still call him Mr Roux. I've never called his wife Robyn. I've always called her Mrs Roux. That's one reason why our relationship has always been very good. I always think that in business or at work it is not right to become too friendly with your boss. If Mr Roux needs to tell me something, he can. It's no problem. If I need to fight back, to give my opinion, I can also. Our relationship is very, very strong.'

It always has been. Within months of Diego joining The Waterside there was a need for honest communication. 'The first thing I noticed when I came here was that it was so French. So, so French. The first thing to do, obviously, was assess the place.'

Diego's assessment was that attitudes to customer service had to change or he would have to leave. Michel Roux was keen to avoid the latter and Diego was given permission to do whatever was necessary to create the required change in the culture of the business. The new philosophy was to be based entirely on Diego's commitment to service, on his unswerving belief that a restaurant exists to serve its customers, not vice versa. However, not all the staff shared this approach and Diego remembers it as a difficult time.

'The first thing you do is you look at your team. You speak to them if you need to, once, twice. If you see that things don't really change, then you change your staff. It's not easy. You have to make hard decisions. So that's what I did. It took me about six months. I changed I would say about 40% of the team. The most important thing to realise is that you cannot do this by yourself. You have to have at least one or two people in the team who think like you. It's not just that they work like you – anyone can be trained to do that – they must believe in the same things. So I offered some people I knew a job and they followed me here. I believe in teamwork. You have to have the right people.'

Within six months the changes were obvious. Michel was delighted with the results. He recognised, too, that his restaurant manager had a very different skill set from his own. Whilst Michel preferred the control of the kitchen, Diego was at home in the restaurant charming even the most difficult of guests.

'Mr Roux could never talk to them easily,' Diego remembers. 'He always asked me, "How can you deal with these people? How can you talk to them?" I always said to him that everyone has at least a little good inside. You have to find it.'

According to Diego, leadership is a lonely role that requires both self-control and commitment. 'If you are a leader, no matter how much pressure you face, you always have to be in control.

If the team see the boss lose control everything crumbles. It's the end of it. So, if you are the leader, never show you are stressed, never show your anger, never show that you are tired. You always have to be 100%. Every morning when I arrive here I must be 100% even if there is a problem. Even if I didn't sleep last night...'

Despite his own work rate, Diego encourages all of his staff to 'stick to their hours'. He believes that it is a mistake for leaders to expect everyone in their team to work the same hours as themselves.

'I always tell them "Don't be like me in terms of hours", because if, as an employee, you see your boss is always there one hour before you and is always staying one hour or more after you, it can be de-motivating. As an employee you feel that you can never catch up with your boss. This is a bad feeling. So, I make clear to everyone if I come here early or stay late it is just something I do for me. I do not expect them to copy me.'

This is more than just a motivational technique, though. Diego argues also that there is a direct relationship between the number of hours an individual works and the quality of their output.

'Personally I think if you want a person to perform at his best, you have to get the right hours of work. Obviously, if you work for sixteen hours every day, for ten to twelve hours you will be productive. The other four you will be less so. We need to get the balance right.'

It is a balance he says he has got right for himself. Others, though, might disagree. 'My day off is Monday. So I come here on a Monday to do my paperwork. But I can still enjoy half my day at home with my family and that is very important. I can switch off. Some people cannot switch off at all and I have learnt to do that.'

His motivation for learning to do so is significant. Unexpectedly, whilst in India, Diego suffered a heart attack. It took him by surprise. 'I've had all sorts of things related to stress and tension, not merely physical things. I didn't recognise it at the time, but the body tells you.'

His health scare was not the only sacrifice that Diego has made in his continual commitment to the Roux dynasty. Brilliance, it seems, comes at a price. 'It's a lot of sacrifice. When my children were six or seven I remember sometimes I would go home for an hour in the afternoons and then come back to work and they used to cry saying, "Daddy, stay at home!" It hurts your heart, but you have to go. I work eleven months of the year, non-stop. I see my Mum and Dad once a year in January, which is my one holiday. Obviously going out with friends is nearly impossible.

'My greatest regret is that I was not there when my children were born and the day after my wife came home from the hospital I had to come to work. It was a Saturday. Mr Roux was not there, so I had to come. The main reason why I have succeeded is my wife Kerry and my two girls Isabella and Francesca. They have always supported me and never interfere with my very demanding profession. I honestly think that when I married my wife I won the lottery.'

For Diego it is neither possible nor appropriate to create deep friendships with members of his team. After all, he is the boss – and twice the age of many of them. For them he always has a role to play, just as he does for his guests. 'Sometimes I look at the reservations book and I see there are eighty guests and I know that thirty are not just coming here for the restaurant, but also to talk to me.' The restaurant is, he says, the place where he feels most relaxed, the place where he does what has always seemed most natural to him. His inspiration, he confides, was his mother.

'She taught me by her example about the importance of service. Whenever I needed something, she was always there ahead of me. She always seemed to know what I needed before I had to ask.'

Diego was born in Oleggio, a small village near Stresa in Italy. Inspired by his mother's example and with the support of his teacher at catering school he moved to France at the age of seventeen to work in Alain Chapel's Michelin-three-star restaurant. It was to be a challenging and lonely time for the young Italian.

The restaurant was in the village of Mionnay, twelve miles outside the city of Lyon. It was a world-famous establishment, owned and run by a chef who was acknowledged as one of the greatest of his generation. It was a wonderful opportunity for a teenage boy who had already decided that he would make a career for himself in the world of fine dining. And yet, as an inexperienced Italian, Diego was not allowed to work in the restaurant during service. Instead he was required only to organise the empty green and brown bottles ready for collection. Living apart from his family for the first time, in accommodation that was several miles away from the restaurant, Diego found the isolation and the long hours stressful. He remembers travelling back to his room in the early hours of the winter mornings struggling through the intense cold and the snow knowing that, no matter how bad the weather was, he would be making the return journey in a few short hours. It was, he admits, a time in which he cried often. His resolve was tested and yet never beaten.

'My desire to learn,' Diego says when remembering this part of his life, 'was always stronger than my tears.'

Alain Chapel took a liking to the determined young man and instructed him to serve lunch and dinner to the Chapel family every day before the guests arrived and service began. It was at these times that the great chef rewarded Diego's desire to learn, teaching him personally the fine arts of serving and carving. As Diego's ability grew, so did his standing in the French restaurant. He stayed there until 1983 when he joined Le Gavroche in London and was promoted quickly to the role of Chef de Rang. Two years later he moved again, becoming the manager at Le Mazarin, another restaurant owned by the Roux brothers, which achieved a Michelin star within months of him taking charge. From there, following a relatively brief spell working for Michel Roux Snr in California and a return to Alain Chapel's, this time as maître d', Diego moved to The Waterside Inn and the rest, of course, is fine-dining history.

Throughout it all, the lesson he learnt from his mother remained one of his core principles. He continues to measure the quality of his team's performance by asking himself, 'Are they meeting the guests' needs before they are expressed?' If the answer is 'Yes' Diego is, in part, a happy man. For him, service means never having to ask. It should also go unnoticed, unless, of course, the guest wants to talk.

'Too much service is as bad as not enough. Service must be very discreet, formal but at the same time informal. It must always be there but the guest must not see it. If a glass is nearly empty, staff should be aware and ready to act. If guests are talking, staff should leave them alone. We should always be looking and interpreting. Obviously nobody is perfect. If I was perfect I would be up there...' (He gestures heavenward). '...But here we aim to get as close as we can.'

It is this quest for perfection that motivates him.

'If I did the same routine every day I would get bored. This place still gives me a lot of excitement. I think I still have a lot to do here. The day that you say you can't improve any more is the day you should just stay at home and fall asleep. So, for me, there must be improvement every day, even just improvements in small details. You cannot let things fall down. If they fall down it is difficult to get them back up again.'

Diego finds it particularly easy to give the guests his full attention. By understanding the guests Diego can do everything in his power to ensure their needs are met. He is also clear, however, that success is dependent upon teamwork. 'Everyone has a task, a designated task, but on their own they cannot achieve anything. It is a team effort, from the girl who takes the booking to the gentleman who parks your car when you arrive. After all, she is the first person you talk to and he is the first person you see. Throughout service the restaurant staff have to rely on each other. They rely on someone else to serve the water, or the bread, or the food or wine. If they don't work together the final result is not there. Everyone knows we are here to work together.'

Diego provides ongoing training for his team. Sometimes it is of a formal nature: 'We will focus one day on carving or another day on cheese,' he says.

Sometimes, though, he creates something that is unexpected, a problem for his staff to solve. 'If things are going very well it is easy for people to become complacent. So I find little problems for them. It is one way of keeping them on their toes.'

For Diego, attitude is the primary requirement when employing new staff. 'Having the right attitude is very important for us. Some people want the job so much you can feel it when they talk to you on the phone. And at the end of the day attitude is what it is all about. If you don't have the right attitude, in any profession, you will never succeed. You have to be hungry – desperate – to succeed. We all know the technique and we can develop this through training. Anyone can learn these things. Technique is teachable. What I am trying to teach them also, my trick, is to get the right attitude, to understand that serving is pleasing. It is far more than just knowing how to carve meat or select the best wine. We are here to create what the French call *bonheur*, contentment. Serving is all about pleasing people, making them feel happy and good, making them feel comfortable. This is true whether it is in a restaurant or a shop. It is true anywhere.'

When a member of staff demonstrates an interest in, or an aptitude for, one particular aspect of service, Diego is quick to help them develop it further. He will also provide unexpected rewards for those who are doing especially well. He understands the value of providing what he calls 'little incentives'.

'One of my boys has done very well recently so last night I sent him to the Dorchester to eat there. Obviously they charged him almost nothing and when he came back this morning he could have kissed me. The boy was touched. These incentives can be many different things. They can be just extra time off. Or help with their family. It could be helping them to open a bank account, or just taking them home at the end of the evening.'

Diego is careful to ensure that, whenever possible, his staff feel valued and supported. In a successful team, he says, people have to trust each other and be able to trust the leader. Conversely, the leader needs to be able to trust their team. 'I need to trust all of them whether they are seventeen years old or thirty. And, as the leader, if the staff don't trust you, if they don't believe in you, they will not follow you. And then you are by yourself.'

Interestingly, despite their dependence on excellent teamwork, neither Diego nor Alain engage in specific team-building activities with their staff. They feel that, whilst staff training helps improve technique, the actual challenge of service creates the necessary communication, understanding and trust upon which great teams are built. Occasionally, everyone will get together for a social event. 'We do boat trips,' Diego says. 'And sometimes we do paintball with the guns. They sting, but I have to go as well. I have to go because if I don't my team will ask why I am not there.'

Staff are not allowed to drink during working hours. When the week is over, however, late on a Sunday night, many will stay behind to chat and share a drink with Diego and their colleagues. 'They know I always offer them a drink. You know, whatever is left behind the bar, half-bottles and so on that will otherwise be thrown away. Some of the team could leave at ten o'clock and yet they wait until one o'clock, because for them it is the highlight of the week. And I stay with them. I take my tie off and open my shirt. We talk about work, sport, cars, and all the other things that young people like to talk about. I would love to go home, but for me it is the best time of the week to build the team.'

Diego's commitment to developing his team is, ultimately, a reflection of his commitment to the business. The maestro in the restaurant never forgets the need to make the required profit. 'Everybody says to me that I have two personalities. Maybe it is because I am a Gemini.' He says this with the same smile that he shares with the guests. 'The team must know that I am on their side, but also I have to think always like a director of the company. I have to run the place as a business.' Which is why, when everything else is done, he retires alone to his office to balance the books.

It is why Frédéric Poulette says, 'It is true, Mr Diego has two faces. He has the face with the customers – smiling, gentleness, everything. And then, you know, he can have another face... The great thing is that, even if you don't agree with him fully, at least 95% of what he says is always right. And he always explains things in a way that you have to agree with. Mr Diego is always one step ahead. I try to be one step ahead of everyone else, but he is always ahead of me. People here respect him so much. You don't want to disappoint him, to feel that you have let him down.'

It is also why Alain Roux once said, 'I would nominate Diego as my hero. I do not know how he copes with so many different customers expecting different service, different care and attention. He not only figures it out, he does more than any customer would expect and the way he does it is natural. Nothing is ever too much for him.'

iii) Building a salad

It is 12.50pm and in the kitchen one member of the team is creating the salad that accompanies one of The Waterside's signature dishes, grilled rabbit fillets served on a celeriac fondant with glazed chestnuts and an Armagnac sauce. It is a simple salad of leaves and dressing and yet it is being put together with care and precision, each leaf being placed deliberately according to its taste, colour and texture. In his autobiography, *Life is a Menu – Reminiscences and Recipes from a Master Chef*, Michel Roux wrote, 'Each salad leaf is different. It might be crisp, or more delicate and smooth in texture. It might be spicy, bitter or sweet. There are as many tastes as colours and the vinaigrettes that go with them should be adapted to suit.'

In the kitchen the building of a simple salad takes far more work and time, structure and sequencing than a guest might ever imagine. The daily routines, schedules and rituals that affect every member of staff are equally deliberate and purposeful. Attention to detail is paramount. Diego focuses on every aspect of front of house. Alain focuses on his brigade of chefs and the processes within the newly refurbished kitchen.

It is a refurbishment that cost one and a half million pounds. The kitchen was gutted and space usage was rationalised, the aim being to increase effectiveness and efficiency whilst maintaining and encouraging the sense of team spirit regarded by both father and son as essential in the running of a great kitchen. Prior to its completion, Alain explained why it was so important to begin again, in effect, and create a new kitchen, 'It's an old building; the walls are uneven and the kitchen's not square or even rectangular – lots of corners... there's only so much you can do with a higgledy-piggledy floor plan. We are going to get rid of that and have pretty much an open space... and clearly defined areas.'

Essentially the change has been one of the inevitable consequences of an increasingly successful business. The Waterside Inn is much busier now than it was in the early years.

'In those days it was a lot more seasonal,' Alain says. 'You'd get quiet weeks in the winter months, although not at weekends. But these days, having rooms, that doesn't happen. I would say we run the business more or less at full capacity all year round... People don't wait for a weekend, or summer, to go away and have a little holiday.'

Michel confirmed the changing trend. 'We do roughly 30,000-32,000 covers a year now – what I needed in the 1980s and what he needs to use now... well, that's completely different.'

What hasn't changed is the sense of tradition and the associated hierarchy. The names of the business and of both Michel and Alain have been engraved above the pass; the staff are, quite literally, working underneath the Rouxs.

Outside the kitchen Diego is engaged constantly in managing and maintaining what he refers to as a 'difficult chain', the relationship between quality, service and profit. He negotiates for the best prices on products. He plans for the future. There is a very strong business ethic in operation that underpins the creation and sharing of *bonheur*. Diego begins most days by checking with the housekeeping staff that everything is in order and by identifying and addressing any maintenance issues. When he has greeted the rest of the staff he meets with his secretary to go through reservations and ensure that any special requests or requirements can be met. He signs personally any letters that have to be sent and then meets with Alain to discuss menus and meals. With this done, he visits reception to deal with any current messages before moving on to the restaurant. It is the place he describes as 'my toy, my playground. It is where I can relax.'

The front of house team prepare the restaurant in near silence. Cutlery and glasses are checked for cleanliness and positioned precisely. There is a sense of calm and purpose that is in some way reminiscent of the preparations in a holy building prior to a very different kind of service. Here, now, ritual combines with practicality. Everyone knows the role they have to play precisely. They go about their tasks with a practised ease that speaks of endless repetition and experience and yet they do so in a manner that suggests the importance of a special, unique event. The room offers the promise of peace on a gentle undercurrent of controlled urgency. This is preparation before performance of the very highest order. And it is like this whether Diego is in the room, whether he is watching, or not. Today he observes briefly and completely before moving on.

After a brief conversation with the sommelier Diego checks that everything is as it should be in the garden and then turns his attention to the reservation book. Diego maintains sole responsibility for allocating tables to guests. It is a task he takes very seriously, regarding it as an essential part in managing the guests' overall experience.

By around 11am Diego is ready to have his own lunch. Whilst he eats he reads a newspaper, updating himself on politics, current events, sports, entertainment and any other topic that guests are likely to raise when talking to him. He insists that his restaurant team can also talk about far more than the menu or the wine list. Although not everyone who visits the restaurant wants to engage in conversation with the staff, those who do need to be accommodated professionally and elegantly.

Diego says, 'Guests like to talk and there's only so much you can talk about the food, the weather and the ducks. They want to talk about politics, about geography, about the economic state of the world. So you need to have knowledge and I drill into my staff how important it is to read. You cannot buy knowledge, you have to work at it.'

It is at the pre-service briefing that Diego shares with the team the knowledge they need to have about who is eating with them, their names, where they will be sitting, their reasons for being there, and any special dietary requirements. He also reviews the team's most recent performance, providing constructive criticism and praise as required. There is no discussion. There is no debate. Staff stand silently in a semi-circle, speaking only when asked a question. Diego switches languages effortlessly and swiftly as he communicates with individuals from different countries. It is not the only change in his delivery. The pace, tone, volume and energy in his voice reflect the fact that the briefing is the final part of the team's preparation. His language is precise, to the point, focused only on the upcoming service and the standards he expects. It is the clipped language of clear direction, stripped of all non-essentials, seemingly impossible to misunderstand. It is the language that is used throughout each service, when time for communication is minimal and yet constant information sharing is paramount. The staff make their notes. The briefing ends. It is almost time to begin.

iv) *Bonheur*

The Waterside Inn is at the end of an appropriately quiet road that leads only to it and the River Thames. What appears to be a single understated white building is actually at the heart of a collection of buildings that incorporate eleven bedrooms including two suites, and a private dining room. The Waterside is a world in miniature with the restaurant at its core. It is a world that works to its own beat with little, if any, regard for what is going on elsewhere in the culinary universe. It is a world of limited size and of great depth, which draws the visitor in, using both man-made and natural boundaries to distance those inside from whatever they have left behind.

From the moment guests step out of their car and hand over their keys to Oliver, the quite literally long-standing doorman, they are beginning a journey of few steps and many layers.

Greetings from, and interactions with, different staff serve to create a sense of transition and engagement, of movement from the everyday world to another that, whilst inevitably transient, is both complete and compelling in its sense of identity and purpose.

Whether guests enjoy their pre-meal drinks and conversation in the tiny lounge or travel through the building and back out into nature to sit in a summerhouse or on the terracing by the riverside, the world at the end of the road immediately begins to exert its influence. It is an influence that is carefully designed and managed, that is at least as dependent on the attitudes and behaviours of the staff as it is on the gentle emotional pull of its riverbank setting where the only sounds are from the occasional boat passing by and the variety of birds – ducks, geese and swans – that have made this part of the river their home, if only for a while. The terracing is simple. Guests sit with their backs to the restaurant. A single willow tree, several lines of carefully shaped shrubs and boxed flowers provide colour and a natural sense of order, easing man-made design down to the water's edge, encouraging guests to let the river take centre stage. Diego's attention to detail is as obvious here as it is throughout the buildings.

Inside, the reception is small and comfortable. The photos on the wall, reminders of the dynasty and the history of which this place is a crucial part, face the main entrance and have to be passed en route to the restaurant. They are almost impossible to ignore. And, one presumes, deliberately so. If *bonheur* is created through service, comfort and never having to ask; if it seeks to combine quality and the highest of standards with an irresistible sense of enjoyment and ease, it does so here in an environment and culture that feels no need to compare itself with its competition or, indeed, to question its values or traditions. No matter how understated the building or simple the décor, this is an *establishment*. And everyone who works here understands that. Whilst *bonheur* is the core value, the raison d'être for The Waterside Inn's very existence, staff serve the heritage of which they are a part as fully as they serve their guests.

Here the gastronomic revolution that Michel and Albert Roux created and led has given way to an equally deliberate evolution. The changes that are happening now are subtle and gradual. Those guests who have been dining here for decades, who bring their children here to be married, who sometimes ask Diego to be a Witness at the wedding, might argue that The Waterside continues much as it always has. Yet Diego is always alert to guests' changing attitudes, knowledge and expectations. And he leads and directs his team accordingly. Whilst many of Michel's classic dishes are still on offer, Alain has been slowly introducing his own and making changes to the richness of the ingredients used. There is now also a tasting menu, the *Menu Exceptionnel*, alongside the set menu and the range of à la carte options. These gentle adaptations, reflecting the ongoing desire for continual improvement, exist because *bonheur* requires it.

Guests dine in the restaurant overlooking the river or in the private dining room, with its walls covered by some of Michel Roux's private art collection and with a private garden to enjoy when the weather permits. If they stay overnight Diego ensures that their breakfast is of the same quality as their dinner, and that their subsequent departure is managed as attentively as their arrival. Diego understands fully the importance of endings. Between the ending and the beginning, though, there is at least one meal to enjoy.

v) The Quiet Man

In the kitchen, Alain Roux, the Quiet Man, leads his team through lunchtime service. It would be an error to mistake Alain's quiet approach for a lack of authority, to presume his calm manner reflects a lack of awareness.

'The chef needs to be in control,' he says, making an immediate connection with Diego's musical metaphor. 'It's a bit like an orchestra. In the kitchen if the chef loses the plot, that is it – the whole team fails. You have to make sure that you are in control. You have to have vision and great timing. Timing is crucial. And the most important thing is communication from the front of house to the kitchen. Sometimes it's only a word or two, but that's what we need. In other professions teams don't always see the "other side of the curtain", but we need to. To be successful we have to know why front of house is working in a certain way and they have to understand why we are.'

The atmosphere in the kitchen reflects Alain's manner. Everyone is quiet, calm, focused. Communication is hushed. He is, he knows, the role model. He sets the tone, the example for his team to follow. He needs to be congruent every preparation, every service, every day. Alain Roux might not attract the media attention that his father does. Indeed, he might not want it. Here, though, in the near-silence of his newly refurbished kitchen, he gets precisely the attention he wants.

'I believe the kitchen should be a calm and disciplined place. I must set the example. The team are trying to give so much, so if I want to keep everyone working to their maximum I have to stay calm myself. I have to be very quick and fast and find a solution if it is needed, but always remaining calm. If I behave in the wrong manner the rest of the team will follow and that will lead to problems on the plate.'

Surely some days his patience is tested, his apparent tranquillity threatened?

'I guess you have your choice. I have my bad days like everybody. In any profession you have to give 100% if you want to be at the top. You have no choice. If you can't do that, how can you have people working with you and tell them to aim for it?' The chef/patron glances down and a half-smile flickers briefly as if remembering a recent challenge. 'Of course, I am only human. However, what can I do? This is my life. I have to be this way.'

And he is. Even with those guests who believe his father is still in the kitchen, who are surprised to know that he, rather than Michel, has just cooked for them. 'Some diners still do not know who Alain is,' Diego says with just a hint of irritation in his voice. 'They do not realise that he is in charge now. Still, he is always calm, always polite.'

Watching Alain Roux move through the restaurant, greeting

guests, talking about his food, *their* meal, it is easy to see why some people fail to realise just who he is. Here, the calm demeanour is coupled with what appears at first glance to be a self-effacing modesty. He listens to the guests' comments, their occasional evaluation, with a thoughtful respect. He is grateful for their praise and quick to divert it away from himself. He is always happier talking about the abilities of those who work for him than of himself.

Yet this is the man who managed the significant and inevitable pressure that came with taking over from a perfectionist parent with a worldwide reputation. He is the man who has maintained the standards and status of a business that is more a part of the establishment than simply well-established. He has managed to combine the traditional nature of the place with a sense of natural growth. He is a man who, at the age of forty-two, was married in the South of France on a Monday evening and was back at work in his kitchen on the Wednesday.

If he keeps his own counsel it is most probably because he chooses not to share, rather than having nothing to say. He prefers the reputation of the business, the food and the guests' experience, to speak for him. Would you select this man to lead a revolution? Almost certainly not. However, his patient achievements imply the self-belief and inner strength essential for all leaders. His control of the kitchen team stems from his own high level of self-control. It is a quality both he and Diego feel all leaders must possess.

Whilst Diego might not believe in the human capability to achieve perfection he is clearly captivated by its pursuit. Perhaps all three men are united by this elusive goal? Alain is clear about what they are seeking to create. 'Every day, every table, every individual guest, we have to perform to the highest standard.' He says it simply, with a slight shrug of his shoulders. 'It is exciting. It is a pressure. It is part of the job. It is very difficult to get to the top, but to stay there is the hardest.'

It is a challenge that both he and Diego appear to enjoy. They share common goals and common philosophies. To them, previous triumphs count for nothing because every service demands their complete attention. Every day is new. There is always much to do and much to learn.

Diego finds it particularly easy to give the guests his full attention. By understanding the guests Diego can do everything in his power to ensure their needs are met. By meeting and talking to the guests Alain gains valuable insights into how well they are performing.

'You have much to learn from your customers,' Alain says. 'Just by the way they are dressed, by the way they express themselves, or their way of standing. Are they here for business or a celebration? Are they with friends or someone they don't know very well? Diego is able to tell all of this. This is the skill of knowing what the customer is here for and what they are expecting.'

And for his own part?

'The reason I come out into the restaurant is to get feedback and to understand and learn about guests; to know what they are looking for in terms of service, food, drink. Every little comment is useful. Over time they become more than just customers. You share many things with them. They see you change and give you their thoughts. Feedback is very, very important. A lot of my key people in the kitchen might not go round the restaurant as I do but they see people when they come into the kitchen. The kitchen team take a lot more heart and pleasure when they know who they are cooking for.'

Both Diego and Alain stress that great teamwork and great communication are essential ingredients in achieving and maintaining excellence. Alain believes that knowing how to communicate and lead well can be achieved in two ways.

'You are born with it or you learn it through experience. Diego is one of those people who are born with it.'

In both the front of house team and the kitchen team, specialists are required to demonstrate their own expertise and to work collaboratively. During service, information has to be shared within and between the teams in a concise and timely manner. Preparation, in both the restaurant and the kitchen, is crucial to a successful service. And yet team members have varying levels of experience and skill. Not everyone understands, nor is expected to understand, the full complexity of the operation.

Alain explains, 'When they start in the kitchen and they are young they need to focus on only one thing at a time. Later they can broaden their focus. When they become senior they definitely get involved in that communication from front of house. Then they are thinking of the whole meal and the entire customer experience.' He goes on, 'In the front of house and the kitchen everything is divided into little sections, everyone has their job to do. Saying that, there are some people who must be able to do more, who must be available and flexible. Of course, there are some who still need to learn how to do that. We don't expect that straight away or from an early age. We make sure that they learn and develop that confidence.'

Alain and Diego agree that great teamwork is dependent in part on the leader creating the right atmosphere. 'When you have got 20 chefs working together,' Alain observes, 'if one of them is not kicking the ball the right way all the others suffer. So it is important to make sure that the heat in the kitchen doesn't become too stressful.'

The leader, he argues, has to have a strong sense of self-belief allied with high-level skills in order to create and maintain such influence. 'You need to believe in what you are doing first. You need to have had enough experience. You have to feel confident and make sure you are a good team player. You have to share everything – sometimes even the bad a little bit. If there is a problem, though, I always take the blame. When things are good, of course, you have to share everything. Most importantly, you have to make sure that everyone understands why they are here.'

Training and motivating the staff, making sure they understand fully the philosophy and purpose of The Waterside Inn, is another vital aspect of the leaders' role here. Again, Alain and Diego lead by example. Alain, as ever, avoids mentioning his own level of expertise.

'I think I've been lucky to have a good education. Something

I have learned from my Dad is that the Chef should always keep learning and should always remember that he is not cooking for himself. You are cooking for your customers. I think in every business it is the same. If you produce something it is not for you, it is for your customers. Sometimes, certain dishes you can develop so far, but you cannot be too crazy and if people give me remarks that are not too positive then I might make changes. You always have something to learn. You never stop learning.'

In the kitchen, Alain has maintained the classics created by his father. 'You have to respect my Dad. Even though I have taken over I have not changed many things. Some others in my position might have changed many things, but I don't think my father would have accepted that and I want to pay respect to what he has done. Also, when something is very good why change it? Sometimes it is too easy to think that when something has been going on for a long time or it is old that it cannot be good – but it can.'

However, whilst respecting the standards and tradition established at The Waterside Inn, Alain has gradually made his own mark, introducing dishes of his own, making subtle changes. No one is more aware of this than Diego. 'At the beginning Mr Michel was in the kitchen, morning, afternoon, evening, all the time. And he was there with his big voice. Alain is now in the kitchen. Alain is a great man. The food has changed. His sauces are slightly lighter. His presentation has changed. His flavours are more pronounced than before.'

For Alain the fact that he is responsible for what is essentially a family business, is also significant. 'There are so few family businesses around the world so if we have a chance to make one last, why not? I think it's great. My Dad and I worked together for ten years. Now he looks after the financial side of the business. He is also a great teacher. He gives me great feedback.'

He does admit though that, on occasion, father and son have had to 'close the office door' when discussing changes to the menu. It is hard to imagine Alain ever raising his voice, easier to imagine him being persistent. Even with the man he calls his 'inspiration'.

As the party celebrating twenty-five years of three Michelin stars neared its end, Alain, Michel and Robyn shared a quiet, intimate moment. Michel was enjoying a cigar and a glass of his much-loved Yquem. Alain wanted to know what his father thought about the food he and his brigade had produced for their distinguished guests.

'Was any dish not too good?' he asked. 'Not as it should be?'

Michel looked his son in the eyes. 'Do you want me to open my heart? Do you want me to be tough? I can be tough.'

Robyn's arm snaked protectively around Alain's shoulders. 'Stop it!' she chided her husband. 'You can be so mean!'

Alain smiled as his father nodded his agreement. 'I can be mean, but do you know the problem? Tonight I have no room, no reason, to be mean.' His gaze never left his son as he continued, 'You have done fine. You have done fine.'

'I need to take that and share it with my team,' Alain said quietly.

It was Michel's turn to smile. 'You know if we had to do it again, what would we change? Nothing. It's my night. It's our night. And I'm proud of my son. So, well done, my boy.'

Alain received the compliment in his usual way. He returned it. 'Well done to you, too,' he said, simply.

It was a rare moment when the highest levels of professional praise were shared between the closest of family members, when the founder of a revolution acknowledged the inevitability of evolution, when the success of change was measured through the maintenance and progression of the status quo. It was one valuable part in the ongoing transmission of a heritage and a legacy.

Outside, in the darkness, the river continued its timeless flow.

vi) Plus ça change, plus c'est la même chose

The history of the Waterside Inn suggests that although change is inevitable, whether it is the result of the obvious, attention-demanding energy of revolution or the more gradual and delicate strokes of evolution, in one sense nothing really changes at all.

The argument expressed so beautifully in the French language, that 'The more things change, the more they stay the same', seems appropriate on several levels when considering the lessons we can take from this iconic establishment.

At The Waterside Inn tradition wraps more than just a cosy arm around the shoulders of modernity. Here, tradition is far more than an excuse for the continuation of well-worn habits, for the justification of mindless repetition because 'that is the way we have always done things around here'. Rather it is at once the heartbeat and the cloak of the establishment. It is the cultural core that determines both how people think and feel when working there and the ways in which the organisation presents itself to the public. This is a culinary heritage site. It is the working home of one half of the family that led the most significant change in British gastronomy. The power of the organisational culture is so great because it is a continuation of that history. And, like all great cultures and histories, they are both regarded as being of far more importance than any one individual.

The leaders of The Waterside Inn seek out, and respond to, feedback and yet they and many of their customers look to the future with one eye fixed firmly on the past. The time for revolution is long gone. The nature and type of change that is taking place now reflects both the personalities of those leading it and the demands of the current context.

This context has been, and is, determined by the power of significant others, including individuals and organisations (particularly those such as Michelin who assess and reward standards), the expectations of customers and the culture of the organisation itself. The importance of creating and then managing the right type of change is emphasised in this story. The value of doing this from the foundation of a powerful, accepted and widely acknowledged cultural base is also clear. Whilst some practices and even the nature of some products might change, the essential beliefs, values and purpose do not.

If the relationship between change and continuity is a form of paradox, so, too, is the relationship at the heart of the other lessons we can draw. It is the relationship between the importance of appropriate power-sharing and the loneliness of leadership.

The Waterside was created and continues to be run by powerful individuals. They have all had to learn how to manage the benefits and challenges of leading a family business that aspired to and achieved the highest accolades. The transition from father to son was a gradual, carefully managed affair. The distribution and sharing of power has been based on personal experience and expertise. Those who are best capable of taking responsibility for specific aspects of the business, do so. Communication between them all is constant and clear, open and frank, and yet it is delivered within and through clearly established boundaries. Everyone here knows their place in the structure. This is as true for the leadership as it is within the kitchen and front of house teams. And it is these boundaries, existing and operating at all levels, that serve to isolate the leaders, to emphasise the fact that they are *of* rather than *in* their team. Both Alain and Diego stress the need for leaders to be available to everyone around them whilst also being removed sufficiently to be able to see the big picture, to take control, to provide, manage and measure direction.

This sense of remoteness is not, it seems, the only price to be paid if one is committed to the acquisition and maintenance of excellence. Family life, friendships, potentially even personal wellbeing, might all be traded in support of corporate realities and dreams, in pursuit of a perfection that can, arguably, never be imagined fully, let alone brought to life. No matter the impossibility of this ultimate goal, the daily requirement is to repeat, learn and, if possible, improve. *Bonheur*, the evidence suggests, comes at a price. For guests that price is listed in the menu. For staff it is more complex. It is determined by their levels of personal commitment, by their personal and professional aspirations and the balance between the two that they are willing to accept in their service of Service.

In conclusion it is clear that, at The Waterside Inn, the purpose of gradual, continual improvement, of never-ending attention to detail, of gathering and responding to feedback, is to maintain what they already have. The world at the end of the road has nowhere else to go and, it is easy to imagine, there is nowhere else it would want to be.

PART TWO

Essential Ingredients

Five Essential Ingredients

'Concentrating on the essentials. We will then be accomplishing the greatest possible results with the effort expended.'

Ted W. Engstrom

Introduction

Welcome to the second part of the book. The stories are over. Now the focus is on the overarching lessons common to all three restaurants.

I begin by explaining why I think of these five lessons as essential ingredients. Then I address each one in turn. Each is made up of several core elements. I have sequenced the ingredients as I have because I believe that some are prerequisites for others.

You might, of course, ask if there really are only five essential ingredients for business success and if not why did I choose these five? The answer is that yes, I believe there are other essentials – great financial management would be one, for example – and I chose these five because it seems to me that these are the ingredients that come first, the ingredients upon which the others depend. Finances do always need to be managed well and yet you are more likely to be financially successful if you get these five ingredients right. And, of course, the book is called *Five Essential Ingredients for Business Success*, not *The Five...*

As for the learning, well, there are many different ways lessons can be structured and shared. I have chosen not to include activities or questions in favour of letting you focus on those topics that are most personally relevant. So, as you read these chapters, do let yourself think about how they can be applied to your situation; do take this opportunity to learn from the experience of some exemplary others. After all, as Goethe wrote, 'All intelligent thoughts have already been thought, what is necessary is only to try to think them again.'

Essentials

The purpose of this investigation was to identify the essentials that have led to the very significant successes of three great restaurants and then to discuss these in ways that highlight their value to organisations within and beyond the hospitality and catering industry. If, as Warren Bennis argued, truly meaningful insights can only be found by studying those who are exemplary, it seems reasonable to believe that knowledge gathered from such a study can be transferred across boundaries and can, even if some adaptation is necessary, be applied to improve performance in a myriad of contexts.

The essentials, be they principles, processes, skills or attitudes, are more open to this transference than specific details that belong within a specific context. The essentials are at the heart of the matter. And that is where we are going and staying for the rest of this book.

Ingredients

It is clear from the three businesses studied that, although they each have their own unique lessons to offer, their success is also due to a combination of five essential factors comprising a mixture of attitudes and behaviours, processes, systems and values which they all demonstrate. I have referred to these five essentials as *ingredients* not just because of the obvious restaurant connection, but also because:

1) Like ingredients, the five essentials have to be mixed and applied in appropriate measure if the most valuable creation is to be achieved.

2) Although each ingredient is significant in its own right, once combined they become greater than the sum of their parts.

3) The leaders and managers studied demonstrate the same intuitive, instinctive ability to manage and mix these business ingredients as great chefs do when working with more natural ingredients to create a dish.

Our three restaurants operate through streamlined, effective and efficient systems that require staff to incorporate big-picture awareness and attention to detail. They combine practicality and logic with creation and experimentation. They are brand-conscious, cost-focused and service-driven. They understand precisely what they are selling and how to emphasise its value.

They also inspire more from their staff than just the desire to do a good day's work and produce the required profit margin. The bottom line is of vital importance, and yet there is something more at stake here than just making money. These businesses stand for something. In each establishment there is a sense of purpose that is far greater than any individual, of values to be upheld and demonstrated, of belonging to something that is challenging and rewarding and irresistible in equal measure, of the need for a level of commitment that absolutely blurs the line between one's personal and professional life.

Underpinning all of the strategic planning and daily operations is the first of our five essential ingredients. It is the element from which everything else develops. It is what came first and what will stay for as long as the business exists. It reminds us that a business is primarily a collection of people joined together with a common aim, and that people are driven by emotion, not just logic. We will begin our consideration of the essentials with the ingredient upon which all else depends.

Ingredient No. 1

Find your passion and then build an enduring cause

'A great leader's courage to fulfil his vision comes from passion not position.'

John Maxwell

This ingredient comprises:
- Passion that fuels an emotional, ongoing commitment
- The nature and power of an enduring cause
- Vision. Visionary leadership and the roles a leader can play
- 'Field marshals' who share and support the leader's cause and vision.

Passion

It starts with passion.

Passion exists before the desire for wealth or fame or status and beyond the need for security or support or comfort. The message that rings loud and clear from my study is:

'If you are filled with passion and are willing to commit and learn and apply endlessly, then aim for the stars; if you lack passion, make finding it your priority if you genuinely want to aim for excellence.'

In this chapter we return to Raymond Blanc's assertion that individuals need to 'find their passion'; we are reminded that Diego Masciaga's desire to learn was always stronger than his tears, and that Michael Caines was back at work leading his kitchen brigade only four weeks after a highly traumatic, near fatal accident.

E. M. Forster wrote, 'One person with passion is better than forty people merely interested.' Our teaching stories were about people who have found their passion; who have used, and continue to use, the energy that passion creates to turn their vision into a powerful reality and to bring people together around a common cause.

Businesses that began because of one person's passion are now managed and run by others who share that passion, who have been attracted not just by the nature of the work on offer or the technical skills of the leaders, but by the fire of emotional commitment that burns within them. Individuals with passion can, it seems, act as beacons for those seeking their own emotive, meaningful purpose. One passionate person might well achieve more than forty merely interested people and, by doing so, can also light the spark of passion within others. They are influential by the example they set and that example moves us because of its emotional content. Zig Ziglar, the American author, salesman and motivational speaker observed, 'People don't buy for logical reasons. They buy for emotional ones.' And the same is true when people buy into the cause of a passionate, creative visionary.

The power of passion, this emotional compulsion that drives behaviour, is at odds with the frequently used line 'This is business, it's nothing personal.' For all of the individuals observed and quoted in the previous chapters, their work, the role they play, the vision they aspire to, is most definitely personal. Their commitment to their business, their colleagues and their guests, coupled with their desire for personal and organisational excellence, is, quite literally, heartfelt. When I asked Frédéric Poulette why he continued to work at The Waterside Inn he said, 'I just love it. I can't explain it.' It was a sentiment echoed by others throughout the three establishments.

In the first instance, though, before attracting others to work with them, before the need to recruit teams of staff, before even the formal creation of a brand and the structure of an organisation, those individuals who were to become leaders had to find their passion, their cause, and then create an inspirational vision.

To learn from their experiences we need to answer an important question and then determine the relationship between passion, cause and vision.

The question to answer is, 'How do we find our passion?' According to Raymond Blanc the most important, and obvious, requirement is the willingness to search for it. His belief is that everyone has a passion even if it needs to be discovered, and that life becomes most fulfilling once that passion has been sparked. Sometimes that spark is created by the examples of others. It is certainly true that the leaders credited parents and grandparents with setting an early example. It is equally true that once these interviewees felt their desire growing within them they showed no intention of ever changing their course. Whether it was the desire to cook or to provide face-to-face service, no matter what setbacks they faced or obstacles they had to overcome, their willpower grew commensurate with their passion.

It became clear through our time together that these passionate people shared some common traits. For example, they all prioritised their personal, internal goals. Once they had realised and established their own agenda and used it to create a clear career path lined with specific milestones, they worked relentlessly (and continue to do so) to achieve the goals they set for themselves. They all identified the specific strengths they needed to develop in order to become outstanding in their chosen field and made the commitment to achieve them no matter what the price. They all very quickly came to associate their professional role and ambition with their sense of personal identity.

And, interestingly, despite the powerful set of internal standards and beliefs they all possess, these leaders also demonstrate an inherent ability to find motivation through appropriate external sources.

People with an external orientation need feedback, outside direction and the opinions of others to stay motivated. Those with an internal orientation provide their own motivation from within themselves; they might gather information and yet they invariably come to their own conclusions about it. Perhaps the hierarchical nature of restaurants means that people who choose to work in them find it easy to accept direction and feedback from significant others. Perhaps the role of chef or restaurant manager appeals only to those who ultimately want to take responsibility for setting their own standards and making their own judgements. Whatever the reason for their combined motivational traits, and whatever the source of their passion, the emotion that led to the creation and success of each business and which continues to be the heartbeat at the centre of them, is clearly a powerful, motivating force which needs to be controlled and directed if it is to create value.

Diego Masciaga made the point that, 'Anyone can be great for a few days.' The real challenge, he believes, lies not in creating an exceptional standard but in maintaining it and, indeed, improving it continually throughout the life cycle of the business.

This is a challenge that appears to be welcomed rather than simply accepted. There is a competitive nature to the managers, teams and, therefore, the cultures of the three restaurants. Only for the most part this leads to a competition that is internally directed, a competition with self – in both a personal and a corporate sense.

It was both fascinating and illuminating to see organisations that are continually reviewed and assessed by external bodies, that are expected to carry the level of the latest measurement in their marketing materials, and that are continually striving either to improve or to maintain that measure, focus primarily on the challenge of continual self-improvement. The approach shared by all involved was to emphasise their own development and progress, to resist the temptation to change their essential corporate identity or values in pursuit of an accolade.

And there was certainly no sense of competitive rivalry driving behaviours. The internal direction of the competition and challenge was more akin to that of a Zen archer, seeking greater knowledge of self and from that a subsequent increased capability, than a professional sport team seeking to beat others en route to a trophy. Passion, the source of their energy, is managed. It is controlled and directed, used and revealed. The common belief is, 'If we just turn inward and focus on improving what we do, if we dare ourselves continually to pursue perfection, external measurements will take care of themselves and, most importantly, our guests will have a memorable experience.'

It is this overriding desire to serve and please, to do everything possible to exceed expectations, that carries all three restaurants into the day-to-day challenge of their work. Every service and every guest interaction is treated as a unique, never to be repeated opportunity to create something magical. Everyone knows that there is only ever once chance to get it right. To watch staff briefings prior to service, to realise the subtle, continual sharing of information acting as the current along which the entire experience flows, to recognise the mix of hierarchy and procedure, flexibility and freelance, is to be reminded that this level of performance can only be achieved and maintained when skill is matched with passion, when the need of the professional to perform to their best is at least as great as the need of the guests to have a great time. To achieve continuing excellence, then, passion has to be directed into a compelling cause.

Cause, caring and commitment

I spent much of 2011 writing a communications book, *Campaign It!*, with the leading campaigner Alan Barnard.[1] For him the notion of cause was central to the need for, and the process of, campaigning to create influence. Indeed, he argues that without a cause there can be neither reason nor impetus for a campaign. In *Campaign It!* we wrote:

'Our modern word *cause* comes from the Latin *causa*, meaning *reason*, *motive* or *lawsuit*. It became part of the English language via the Old French word *cause*, which meant either *a cause* or *a thing*... Today most of us use the word as a noun that identifies either:

---

1 *Campaign It!* Published by Kogan Page, February 2012.

i) The source or reason of an event or action

or

ii) A principle or aim that exceeds selfish desires and is worth striving for.

Both of these usages are essential in our approach to campaigning. For us, cause is the pursuit of an outcome, a principle or an aim that will improve at least some aspect of a current situation. Moreover, it is the emotional compulsion to achieve your desired outcome. It provides both the motivation and, when necessary, the courage to campaign. The cause becomes the story you just have to tell. It is something that we feel is worth committing to and working towards and so it becomes the source, or reason, for the creation of a campaign.

Having said that, we need to make an important point:

'Causes range in size and scope. They can be simple, complex, personal, shared. Some causes can be achieved literally in minutes through a campaign delivered in a single communication, some require a handful of communications, whilst others might need complex sequencing and layering of communications and take several years to achieve.'

In the final analysis we decide what is or isn't a cause in our lives. We decide because a cause is identified and defined by our level of care, by how important we believe something is for ourselves, our families, our organisations, communities or world. In the first instance we don't need anyone else to agree with us about the value and importance of a topic. Obviously, it is nice and it makes life easier if we do have a lot of immediate agreement or support, however a cause begins as a personal commitment and develops into a shared purpose...'

In our three restaurants we see many examples of a personal commitment being developed over time into a shared purpose. And these examples stretch beyond just the obvious, well-known leaders. Managers at all levels promote both the cause that drives the business and the very specific processes by which the cause is achieved.

There are a variety of causes demonstrated within each business, including personal, shared, simple and complex. However, they invariably combine in pursuit of the primary cause, that of the creation of a truly memorable experience for all guests. Every member of staff, whatever their role or level of expertise, is made fully aware of the cause that drives the business, of their overall purpose and of the part they play in helping to achieve it. And this awareness is constantly reinforced.

The sense that everyone is working for, and towards, something bigger and more important than any individual – more important, indeed, than any particular team – is created by the seeding of the corporate cause throughout every layer of the organisation. This, in turn, becomes connected to a range of meaningful symbols including buildings, individuals, stories, environments, even the notion of legacy or heritage. In these elite establishments, the sense of cause that first motivated an individual to direct their life along a specific path has become an inescapable part of the culture, a taken for granted, deep-rooted assumption that envelopes all who choose to work there, demanding from them an emotional commitment that is at least as great as their technical expertise.

The ability to share a vision and a purpose is the bridge that links the individual's personal cause with the creation of an accepted and motivational corporate cause. The founders and the current leaders of these restaurants are people who understand absolutely the need to build support, and yet who are also willing to stand alone to pursue and promote their personal ideals. They seem to have implicitly recognised their personal weaknesses as well as their strengths. Consequently, they have recruited the best support to help run the business and created the professional and social recognition needed to attract custom. Congruently, they have realised that the cause they champion is greater even than they are. If human beings have a powerful need to belong, the shared commitment to a common cause meets that requirement in a most significant way.

The enduring nature of the cause created and sustained in each business might be as much to do with the need of the professionals to serve something even more significant than individual guests, as it is to do with the guests' need to make the sharing of food meaningful. In restaurants, as in all other businesses, the satisfaction of a variety of needs is sought whenever customers and staff share a common experience. In restaurants, as in all other businesses, the responsibility for meeting these needs lies with the professionals involved. The emotional buy-in to the cause increases the likelihood that this responsibility will be acknowledged, welcomed and met.

No matter how relevant or potentially powerful any cause is, it can only develop if it gains sufficient recognition and support from inter-related groups. For our restaurants these most obviously include staff, current and potential customers, and assessment and accrediting bodies. Alan Barnard emphasises the need for individuals and organisations to gain the permission of others when seeking to fulfil a cause.

He argues that no matter what the context, desired end outcomes can only be achieved when the permission of appropriate others has been earned. This requires an awareness of who these people are, an understanding of their current perceptions, behaviours, values and needs, and the ability to communicate with them persuasively coupled with ways of measuring the influence being created. This is not a one-off process. Once the cause has gained support and the initial vision has been shared and created, future developments are dependent upon an ongoing understanding of the changing needs, knowledge and expectations of these different groups.

When Diego Masciaga talks of the changes Alain Roux has made to the dishes offered at The Waterside Inn, when Raymond Blanc explains how a question about duvets and blankets spawned a new five-year business strategy, when Michael Caines stresses the continuing relevancy of Gidleigh Park proclaiming, 'This is a marathon, not a sprint,' they are all reinforcing the importance of understanding and responding to the changing needs and attitudes of those people on whom their success depends.

It is the commitment to the continuing nature of this process that turns a passion into a shared cause. Corporate momentum is created through the relationship between passion, cause, permission and vision. It is a momentum that is developed by the ways systems in place release and help develop the capability of the staff. It is a momentum that is directed towards the most current vision – and vision, like all moving targets, is both a motivation and a challenge, an irresistible summons towards the future.

Vision and the necessity of change

John Kotter wrote, 'Effective leaders help others to understand the necessity of change and to accept a common vision of the desired outcome.' The effectiveness of our restaurant leaders is certainly due to their ability to identify what should and shouldn't change and their willingness to develop and share the vision. The motivational vision that compels action, that draws people towards it, combines an interesting mix of apparent opposites.

The first of these is simply this: what begins within an individual has to be expressed, shared and accepted by others if it is to become a meaningful reality. And this transformation through communication highlights the other, interconnected yet seemingly opposite elements. These are:

i) Every vision begins as a piece of fiction, an imagined possibility and, if managed well, becomes a tangible experience that is a part of the accepted culture

ii) Every vision, therefore, by definition draws together the present and the future

iii) The vision is simultaneously inspiring and challenging, appealing and, at times, frightening

iv) The vision is emotional in its appeal and yet dependent upon practicality and timeliness in its application.

For a vision to be most easily understood and for its value to be most easily appreciated, two factors need to combine. These are communication skills and timing. Those advocating the vision need to be accomplished storytellers who know how to construct and deliver a vivid, detailed, motivational and, perhaps, daring view of a desired future, based on an understanding of all significant factors that influence the context within which they are operating. They have to tell a story that makes the benefits to stakeholders clear. It has to identify and justify the organisational structures and systems that will best deliver these benefits and the leadership and management styles, the methods and expressions of control and support, that are most suited for their implementation. Perhaps most importantly, it has to be a story delivered in the language and through the communications channels used by those whose support is being sought. And, given that our world is filled with, and fuelled by, myriad stories, the visionary story has to be worthy of attracting and then maintaining attention.

This is easier to achieve if the vision and the cause that underpins it are being promoted at the most appropriate time and progressed through the appropriate timescale. Timing is as important in this regard as it is in the actual day-to-day operations of the restaurants themselves. Michael Caines's awareness of the transience of creativity, of the need to capitalise on one's 'moment in time', is another reflection of this point. A vision that is current, recognised as being relevant to the needs of society, is likely to gain acceptance and support more easily than one that is less obviously well timed.

For storytellers, timing has always been a vital part of their craft, and it remains so even if the story being told is intended to gain support for a cause and an associated corporate vision, rather than just to entertain. Storytellers also need to share their story with clarity and conviction, particularly if they are championing a significant change or development.

Theodore Hesburgh, President Emeritus, University of Notre Dame, wrote, 'The very essence of leadership is [that] you have a vision. It's got to be a vision you articulate clearly and forcefully on every occasion. You can't blow an uncertain trumpet.' The challenge, of course, is to demonstrate certainty in the face of opposition, apathy or uncertainty, to be able to convince others that your proposed vision of the future is the most appropriate way to progress a specific cause.

Sometimes, for those at the very forefront of industry developments, the challenge is even more basic: it is to convince others of the value of the actual cause itself. The culinary revolution in the UK created and led by Michael Roux Snr and his brother, Albert, is one very obvious example of a significant cultural shift created by an increased acceptance of a previously un-considered cause. Whether such revolutionary leaders need to be courageous is open to debate. Raymond Blanc argues that when passion combines with an instinctive, overwhelming sense that something has to be done, there is no need for bravery. When these forces meet, he says, the need to act becomes irresistible – even if that action creates challenges and incites opposition.

It should be noted, too, that these irresistible actions are demonstrated in different ways, reflections perhaps of the innate personalities of those who choose to campaign a cause. Alain Roux's quiet resolve and his comfort at remaining relatively in the shadows are, for example, in obvious contrast to his father's high-profile leadership. Yet Alain's commitment is as complete as his passion; hidden behind a reserved, at times self-effacing manner, it is all-consuming. Indeed, this is a man so committed to the cause rather than to personal recognition that his role and influence have been realised only gradually by many of those visiting The Waterside Inn. And, as he made clear, he enters the restaurant to meet his guests in search of feedback, not fame.

If there is a glue that holds together vision and cause, it is emotion. In *Campaign It!* we made this point in the following way:

'...a cause is far more than just a detailed and clear vision of the future. The cause is the *why,* not simply the *what.* It reflects values whilst promising value. It is worth striving for because we *feel* its worth rather than just being able to measure its reward. The cause is the story we have to tell now, not the novel we might get round to writing one day. Our cause, whatever it might be, is brought to life by the implementation of the desired end-outcome, however it is born out of our emotional need. It is because of the need for, and power of, cause that we say quite simply,

"If you care enough, campaign it!"'

The individuals who, in this book, speak to us through their words and actions, all care enough. They all have a range of personal causes that support, and are supported by, the corporate cause. And in this joining and sharing of emotion, this absolute desire to create excellence, the role of the leader is paramount.

The leader, the orchestra and the crowd

Jonathan Swift wrote, 'Vision is the art of seeing the invisible.' If that is the case, leadership is the art of making the invisible clear for all to see. In order to achieve this, the leaders I studied played any or all of the following roles:

- Visionary
- Teacher
- Storyteller
- Role model
- Student
- Figurehead
- Fighter
- Servant
- Performer.

As the role of visionary has been discussed, we will begin this brief overview with a consideration of the restaurant leaders as teachers. And we will start by making the point that the leaders within our three restaurants are teachers who have 'gone first'. They are what Alan Barnard calls 'cause-creators', who have become teachers out of necessity. In the first instance they had to identify or create the cause, determining its scope and value, then they had to teach others about the value of their cause and how to turn the vision into an enduring reality. They teach continually so that those around them can achieve the necessary standards and, also, to ensure the development of their industry. Their teaching extends to include the wider population, educating them in some aspects of their professional skills, using this to promote aspects of their cause and attract interest to their business. Their involvement in my study and their support of this book is, arguably, an example of their desire to inform and educate coupled with an awareness of the promotional benefits. It reflects, too, their natural inclination to use stories as a teaching medium and as a promotional device. They are, as I have already indicated, experienced and willing storytellers.

They recognise too that, as teachers, they create influence both through the sharing of knowledge and the formal provision of training, and through the personal example they set. For them, the leader is – has to be – a role model for others to follow and learn from. When Gary Jones at Le Manoir aux Quat'Saisons shares the story of his own learning and transformation from a dominant, some might have said aggressive, chef, into a deliberate and caring mentor, he is acutely aware that he is offering an example that some might need to follow. When Alain Roux says, 'If I behave in the wrong manner the rest of the team will follow and that will lead to problems on the plate,' he is emphasising his power as a role model. The leaders studied know that they are watched as well as listened to. They share a common understanding that some of the most significant lessons they offer derive from their consistent daily behaviour. It is an understanding best summarised by Damien Bastiat's observation that, 'You are teaching whilst you are managing. Acts are more important than words. Staff learn by watching you every day.'

Damien's example is just one of many within this study that highlight the need for a leader who is a teacher and a role model also to be a perpetual student. Without exception, the leaders within the restaurants are fuelled by their own desire to learn and improve. Despite their obvious levels of achievement, the many external accolades and awards, they exemplify the notion that 'the more you know, the more you realise you still have to learn'. Indeed, in many respects, their right to function as teachers and role models is earned as much by their unflagging urgency as students as by their current levels of skill, knowledge and experience. Albert Schweitzer argued, 'Example is not the main thing in influencing others, it is the only thing.' Even if its absolute significance may be open to debate there is no doubting that it does, at least, have an important part to play. And the restaurant leaders are fully aware of that.

They know, too, the importance of a figurehead. This is often a role associated with nominal leadership, a position of profile lacking genuine authority. Our examples, though, combine both profile and power. They understand, too, the symbolic nature and significance of a figurehead. Yet, as with the other leadership roles, they play the part in ways that reflect their own personalities within a deliberately selected range of contexts. Raymond Blanc, perhaps the most obvious example of a figurehead amongst those studied, has created an almost constant media presence, writing books, providing interviews and presenting his own television programmes. He is aware that his audiences inevitably associate him and the way he presents himself with the values and standards of Le Manoir aux Quat'Saisons. He understands fully that in the public perception the individual becomes synonymous with the place, the leader and the business become entwined, the organisation is seen as a reflection of the person and vice versa. It is no surprise, then, that Raymond is a master of sharing his passion, his commitment to luxury and service, his creativity and humanity, through a variety of media. To appreciate the symbolic power and attraction of the leader as a figurehead, one needs to do no more than watch or listen to him in action.

Raymond is not the only figurehead, however. Michel Roux Snr continues to travel the world promoting The Waterside Inn, Michael Caines maintains a high profile and Diego Masciaga's more recent awards reflect his status internationally and enable him to play the role.

In less obvious ways, managers within the restaurants act as figureheads for their particular teams, leading the way by example, cutting through unexpected difficulties or the challenges of change with their commitment to specific values. In this way the role model becomes a type of internal figurehead, exemplifying the character and qualities needed to be successful, drawing emotional support from those who work with them.

Despite their power – or, indeed, perhaps because of it – the leaders also act as servants. Most obviously, of course, they serve their guests. However, they also serve their staff through the many layers of formal training on offer, through informal support and career progression. Julia Murrell exemplified this approach when she talked of the need to treat the staff as guests, saying, 'If we are seeking to provide five-star service to our guests, we need to provide the same level of service to our staff.'

Those with role power also serve the values that underpin each business and upon which they were founded. One of the most important of these is Service.

In an age and society in which the notion of service, of *serving*, appears by many to be increasingly associated with weakness, with a lacking of social status or worth, these leaders challenge the perception with a rigour and a force that some might view as paradoxical. Here, in these centres of excellence, service is at the very heart of the agenda. And the lesson they teach is that truly great service is the result of a myriad of skills developed to the highest levels, applied by exceptional teamwork through the most effective and efficient systems. It is a combination that can only be developed through discipline, effort and self-motivation. Exceptional service, it would seem, is a route most difficult to tread, requiring determination and desire in equal measure, to be chosen only by those with the energy to endure. It is no wonder, then, that those who can operate so comfortably and well as servants, can also play the role of fighter when required.

It is a requirement called for by the competitive environments within which they operate, their own internal desire for continual improvement and the unpredictability of events. Interestingly, none of the leaders used the label 'fighter' when describing themselves, even though they all demonstrated a willingness to pursue their goals in the face of opposition, to defend their staff from inappropriate or unfair criticism, to strive continually no matter what the setbacks. They are fighters who, because of their desire for personal improvement, seem to have realised instinctively that, no matter what the nature of the conflict, the ultimate fight is always with oneself.

Ernest Hemingway wrote, 'The world is a fine place and worth fighting for.' The three restaurants are worlds in miniature. They have been created, maintained and developed by people prepared to fight for them, to champion their worth, to protect and promote their values. These protective instincts serve another benefit, too. They create a feeling of security amongst the staff, who know that their managers will defend them against unwarranted comments and reserve their own constructive criticism for a private moment.

The leaders I observed and met were all performers, capable of combining any, or all, of the above roles according to the demands of the situation. And, of course, they are roles that inevitably overlap. For example, the best teachers are at once visionaries, role models, figureheads and the best of students. They serve, perform and will fight for what they believe in.

In the restaurants, every pre-service briefing is a form of call-to-arms. It is more than just a last-minute talk about strategy and tactics. It is a reminder of the importance of the event, of the raison d'être of the business, of the fact that, just as with any other performance, there will be only one chance to make a positive, lasting impression. It is a bringing together of the team and a focusing of minds, the last few moments before the curtain rises, when leadership is demonstrated and responsibilities accepted.

It is not by accident that Diego Masciaga likened himself to the conductor of an orchestra and that Mourad Ben Tefka at Le Manoir aux Quat'Saisons compared service to a theatrical performance with himself, by implication, as the Director. These descriptors remind us again of the independent nature of leaders, of their desire to accept responsibility, to stand out from the masses to set the style, tempo and pace for others to follow. As James Crook observed, 'A person who wants to lead the orchestra must turn his back on the crowd.' And these leaders do have their faces turned fully towards their vision and their backs turned fully towards anything that does not help them to achieve it.

They cannot, though, create a magical performance alone. The cause endures and the vision is made manifest because of the efforts of the team(s) and, especially, the work of those Raymond Blanc describes as 'field marshals'.

Field marshals, lieutenants and the appropriateness of structure

Raymond's field marshals are those senior managers who understand and share his vision and values. They are entrusted with the responsibility for making things happen and ensuring that standards are maintained and targets met. Diego Masciaga shares Raymond Blanc's view about the importance of such individuals. He also used a military descriptor, referring to them as his 'lieutenants'. Indeed, when Diego faced challenges introducing his approach to service at The Waterside Inn, he not only let staff go, he replaced them with well-known and trusted 'lieutenants'.

The militaristic nature of the language, structure and methods of operating, particularly during service, reflect the intensity of the activity. Staff have to work collaboratively, combining individual expertise, sharing information, responding instantly to any unexpected changes, managing time, maintaining standards and, most important of all, making it seem effortless throughout. When Michael Caines argued for the importance of systems in the production and maintenance of excellence, he was making the point that systems need to be determined by the nature of the activities undertaken and the desired end outcome, not the other way round. Unsurprisingly in all three restaurants the systems, like the staff, serve the vision and the cause, and they are created, implemented and managed by field marshals or their equivalent.

The engagement of such experienced, like-minded supporters is a tactic that is also intended to help speed change, to enable the leader to spend time working strategically, creatively or on specific operational aspects, and to develop or reinforce the culture. These senior managers can also operate as advisors, providing their own thoughts when asked about future plans. Philip Newman-Hall, for example, an incredibly talented and well-regarded manager in his own right, is adept at the roles of implementer and occasional advisor. He, like the others who support their leader in this way, also plays a significant part in the implementation of Ingredient No. 2. It is the next part of the mix, and without it this first element would be ultimately unachievable. It is the importance of a congruent, shared identity.

Summary

The learning points in this chapter are:

1. Passion comes before cause
2. Cause comes before vision
3. Vision begins as a work of fiction that challenges, motivates and attracts
4. Leadership is the art of turning fiction into a valuable, shared reality
5. To achieve this, great leaders play a variety of roles
6. They ensure that the systems in place serve the cause and lead to the desired end outcomes as effectively and efficiently as possible
7. They need 'field marshals' to help them.

One other point to remember: it is essential to maintain an enduring relevance through changing times. As Diego Masciaga and Michael Caines said:

'Anyone can be great for a few days. Success is a marathon, not a sprint.'

Ingredient No. 2

Know who you are and then make sure everyone else does, too

'Make it thy business to know thyself, which is the most difficult lesson in the world.'

Miguel de Cervantes

This ingredient comprises:
- The self-understanding that precedes brand creation
- The role of recruitment, selection and induction in creating and ensuring a consistent corporate identity and an exceptional customer experience
- The need to create the level of team that is most suitable for 'your' operation
- The value of a Learning Culture and how to create it
- Ensuring congruency between internal and external communications.

Self-understanding, identity and a dog with blinkers

Organisations seek to create and share a congruent and engaging identity that spurs both a common perspective and a shared sense of value in the onlookers. They need to know precisely who they are, what they stand for, what they offer and the boundaries within which they operate before they can hope to communicate this to their target market.

One of the difficulties in gaining this level of self-knowledge lies in knowing precisely where to look for the answers. Ann Lander's warning not to 'accept your dog's admiration as conclusive evidence that you are wonderful,' is as good a director as any. Even though the perceptions and opinions of valued others might be called into play, clarity of business identity starts, like charity, at home. And, if Ingredient No. 1 is in the mix, this is a home built by a passion that can potentially blind or, at least, blinker leaders and their teams to their own organisational realities. The requirement to:

1) Know who you are
2) Know how to demonstrate this congruently and consistently

demands an objective awareness in the first instance and a deliberate communications strategy in the second. Knowing your corporate identity incorporates far more than just understanding the needs you are satisfying through the production of specific products and/or services. It also includes the creation, understanding and ongoing management of a specific ethos, the implementation of deliberate strategies, and the use of a range of performance measures. It requires a clear understanding of the industry you are in, the nature of the competition, and your current (and desired) role and status within it.

Demonstrating who you are is done through the creation of the most appropriate corporate culture, the nature and management of relationships with stakeholders, and the use of symbols, logo and associated media, all of which have to be stitched together to form an integrated communications campaign.

The ultimate measure of success in this regard is simply the degree of synchronicity between how you want to be regarded and valued and how you actually are. For organisations, as for individuals, identity is demonstrated. It is the result of actions – and these actions include *words* – perceived and interpreted by others. When Alain Roux talks to diners in his restaurant, when Mourad Ben Tefka claims that 'Feedback is the breakfast of champions', they are both reminding us of the organisational need constantly to seek the power made famous by the Scottish poet Robert Burns – 'to see ourselves as others see us.' The corporate challenge, though, is for all involved to assume responsibility for how the business is perceived, to act in ways that reinforce the agreed organisational identity, to shape the perceptions of others so that they are obliged to see us as we wish to be seen.

To presume that this is achieved solely, or even primarily, through the use of marketing materials is to ignore many avenues through which identity can be introduced, expressed or reinforced. Philip Newman-Hall's observation that Le Manoir's reputation as a centre of training excellence is furthered every time very capable staff members leave to work elsewhere, is just one example of how identity can be transmitted deliberately through apparently indirect means. The lack of a formal reception desk at Gidleigh Park is another. And the role played by Oliver, the doorman at The Waterside Inn, is one more.

Building from our first ingredient, we can come to think of corporate identity as the business embodiment of passion and purpose. And identity has an inevitability that screams loud for it to be developed, directed and managed with rigour and thoroughness. Once an individual or an organisation is in the public domain an identity will be determined. The choice is simple: to leave it purely to the eye of the beholder or to sculpt and shape an identity that cannot be misinterpreted and is undeniably appealing. Actually, of course, there is no choice at all. Identity is the way we express who we are through what we do. Each of our restaurants has absolute clarity about both elements. Indeed, it is because of their very different identities that I was able to write about them in the same book. Though their business success is based on the same five essential ingredients, the ways they mix and use these ingredients is different, and that difference stems from their distinct identities.

They are identities that inevitably reflect the personalities of the founders or leaders, are influenced by their location, and are expressed through a mixture of architecture, systems, products, symbols and people. They are identities that seem obvious and appropriate now and yet took time to develop and establish. David Quammen, the American science and nature writer, said, 'Identity is such a crucial affair that one shouldn't rush into it.' Neither should one avoid it. The passion that led to the creation of these three businesses is a passion for *being* as much as it is a passion for *doing*. Knowing who you are informs knowing how to behave. It means knowing your place in the world and how you uniquely fill the space you have claimed as your own.

In one sense the three restaurants are all the same. They are elite, Michelin-starred establishments seeking to provide the very best cuisine, service, surroundings and overall experience that they possibly can. However that serves only to introduce the stories, not to tell them. These places do fill their time and space in uniquely different ways. Their individual identities stretch out through every parameter of their business. They seek to ensure that every aspect of their buildings and grounds, their processes and interactions, are filled with identity. It is as if their identity projects itself from the inside out. The décor, the setting, the nature of the service, the food offered, the language used all reflect something deeper, something we might think of as the essence of each place and, perhaps, of the people they represent. They behave in the ways they do because of their identity, not in an attempt to suggest an identity. Quentin Crisp wrote, 'Fashion is what you adopt when you don't know who you are.' These restaurants do know themselves. Which is why, in one sense, they are beyond fashion. They are neither fashionable nor fashion-less. Their individual brands succeed regardless of current short-term trends.

Indeed, it is easy to believe that this clear sense of Self is one reason why none of the three regards other restaurants as direct competitors. After all, how can one reasonably compare very different identities? And, of course, when you are focused on becoming a better version of yourself, why waste time on fruitless comparisons with others?

This high level of self-awareness (and self-regard) is reflected in the various ways the restaurants communicate themselves to their target markets. Essentially, all of their communications revolve around the simple expression of their identity. This can be allied closely to a central figure, as is the case with Raymond Blanc, or to a history and a legacy, as is the case with The Waterside Inn. It can highlight any other aspect of the identity story and the associated benefits. The bottom line, though, is that all three created a congruent heartfelt corporate identity before creating a communications strategy.

They are all equally aware that the ways their staff function amongst themselves, with guests, and with other stakeholders, is an integral part of that communication. It is essential, therefore, that all staff know, appreciate and value the identity of the business and recognise that this identity is revealed as much through their behaviours as it is through any formal marketing. The lesson is that the role of recruitment and selection is crucial in being who you are and in then sharing that with others.

Recruitment, rowing and rugged individuality

Before I began my study I imagined that only the most experienced and highly skilled individuals would stand any chance of ever being employed by such world-class organisations. In truth, shared beliefs and values, and a demonstrable passion, were regarded as being of far more importance. Skills, I was told by people within all three restaurants, can be taught. Attitude, on the other hand, cannot. When it comes to recruitment and selection, everyone was in agreement that attitude was the primary quality. The message seems to be: prioritise employing people who share your passion, who are committed to your cause and your methods of achieving it, and then be willing to invest in their development.

Julia Murrell's approach to recruitment and selection at Le Manoir exemplifies this attitude and practice. Here, recruitment processes are used to identify those individuals who best fit the culture and ethos. Induction is then used to make clear the identity of the business and to ensure respect for the work done in every department by providing work experience throughout the organisation. It thus also clarifies the new member of staff's role within the grand scheme of things.

Staff development is an integral part of the culture of each restaurant. Sometimes the training is determined by the managers, sometimes it is requested by specific staff. Sometimes it is presented as a necessity, sometimes as a reward. Sometimes it is formal in nature, sometimes it is informally introduced into the daily routine. Diego Masciaga is a master of this tactic, always willing to create an unexpected problem for his team to solve – just to keep them on their toes. Whatever the reason or the style of the training, though, it remains an inevitability. Individual expertise is highly prized in these establishments. It has a value that is only matched by that of exceptional teamwork.

Exceptional teamwork is at the core of these businesses' success. Earvin 'Magic' Johnson, former basketball superstar and now hugely successful entrepreneur, observed, 'You are only as good as your team.' It is a maxim that could be written on the walls of every dining room, kitchen and office within the restaurants. Only it would be an unnecessary waste of space. No one I met or observed needed reminding about the importance of team. No one thought they could accomplish their mission alone. And everyone was fully aware that they had a responsibility to their teammates.

For over two years I watched an excellence of operation, a level of teamwork that could only be matched, one imagines, by the very best sports teams and elite military. Did I observe absolute perfection? Of course not. After all, these are human beings we are talking about and, as Gary Jones wryly observed, 'Whenever you add human beings to a system…' However, I did see clearly defined and motivated teams working together day after day, month after month, in pursuit of that elusive target. And no one was more critical of their performance, however wonderful the result, than they were. My only regret in all that time was that I lacked the courage to say out loud,

'There might not be an "I" in "team", but there is certainly a "me" "n" "u" in "menu".'

Perhaps in hindsight it's best that I didn't...

Ralph Waldo Emerson, on the other hand, did have the courage to express, 'No member of a crew is praised for the rugged individuality of his rowing.' Interestingly, in the restaurants individuality is demonstrated and, indeed, plays a vital role. After all, these are centres of human interaction. Although the food does need to be outstanding, few would return repeatedly if the level of service were not at least as good. And, when all is said and done, service is simply a descriptor for the interface between customer and provider. However, it is a descriptor that is a verb, rather than a noun. It describes what can be a potentially fluid process during which the professionals at least are making a series of complex judgements, often balancing the requirements of guests and colleagues in a manner designed to keep all happy. In this regard the individuality that is essential to great customer service also seeks to balance the efforts of everyone else involved. What helps to achieve this – and this is one of the many things that everyone in the restaurants takes for granted – is the fact that every team member knows what everyone else is doing. Again, like the most fluid and efficient sports teams, they are reading the state of play, ready to support or pass on information.

What makes these teams very different from those in sport, and from those in many other businesses, is the fact that here there are very different teams working together in tandem. In most organisations product development teams are rarely working so close to the customer service teams that they can pass their product on to them in real time. In all restaurants, not just our elite three, this is an inevitable and crucial part of the operation. The kitchen team and the front of house team are self-contained units that are totally dependent on each other. Their interactions are constant. Each understands fully their value to the other. Great restaurants do not just offer us a demonstration of how one elite team works, but of how elite teams work together. It is through this complex mix of collaboration and individuality, personal excellence and interdependency that they reveal the identity of the establishment.

Their example prompts a question:

'Does every team in every organisation need to be operating at an elite level?'

It is perhaps too easy for leaders, managers and, indeed, team members themselves to claim either a need for, or even the capability of, excellence. Perhaps there is a level of pressure, an insidious form of social proof, that makes us feel obliged to claim or aim for elite teamwork? Perhaps it is as easy and as meaningless a trend as that which has led to every management job specification requiring aspirants to be 'Outstanding Strategists', 'Brilliant Communicators' and 'Motivational Leaders'? When, in fact, to be truly just one of those three requires a lifetime's commitment.

Before this study I had been willingly drawn into the 'Let's aim to be elite' category. Now I have changed my thinking to such a degree that I obviously feel obliged to pose my question. And my own answer is firmly established. It is, 'No. Not only do very few teams need to be elite; very few teams have the capability to be so. And, going one step further, not every group of professionals working together even needs to become a team at any level.'

I would suggest that the questions regarding teamwork that managers need to ask themselves are:

1) Do I need these people to operate as a group or a team?
2) If as a team, then what level of teamwork is required?
3) Once that is determined, how best do I share this
   information with the staff?
   and then
4) How best do we create and maintain the required level of
   teamwork?

5) What other teams, if any, are we dependent upon and how do we best manage our relationship with them?

The answers to these questions will be determined by context and desired end outcome. As simple, working definitions, a group can be regarded as a number of people who are aware of each other, possibly sharing some things in common, engaging in some form of interaction. A team, however, is a group that is deliberately created and managed to achieve specific goals. A group might share some common interests or desires. A team is bound by values and beliefs. However, the values that bind do not guarantee any level of capability. They might play an important role as motivational forces, but they do not ensure individual skill or, for that matter, team coordination. These things are based on the quality and appropriateness of recruitment and selection processes and enhanced through staff development.

The most obvious way to determine the level of teamwork needed is by understanding fully the nature of the activities they are required to perform and the vision towards which they are travelling. Critical factors might include:

- The expectations of key stakeholders
- The time frame and the importance of time management
- The degree and nature of challenges to be faced
- The degree and level of competition
- The agreed definition of success
- The agreed definition of failure
- The number of errors the process can sustain before failure occurs
- The need for high levels of individual expertise
- The need for high levels of communication between experts, including accurate and timely information-sharing
- The levels of control that can be exerted upon each aspect of the process and, equally, the degree of unpredictability.

Interestingly and, perhaps, surprisingly the restaurants I

studied do not emphasise specific team-building activities. They would argue that they need an elite level of team performance because:

- The expectations of guests are exceptionally high
- The expectations of staff to exceed these expectations are even higher
- Everything is dependent on exceptional time management
- They do recognise that their guests can choose to spend their money on an extensive range of other luxury products and services
- Their definitions of failure are precise and acute; there is no tolerance for error
- Everything is dependent on individual experts performing to their best
- Everything is dependent on collaboration and exceptional communication and information-sharing between these experts
- There is the inevitable unpredictability associated with interacting with, and managing, guests
- They have the highest of reputations to maintain
- They are judged publicly and frequently
- They are judged by their latest performance.

However, the restaurants argue, too, that for the most part the actual process of managing service twice a day and the subsequent debriefings develop and maintain the necessary standards. Time spent undertaking other team-building activities is, therefore, not needed.

Perhaps, then, it is as simple as this: if you don't require people to work together collaboratively in time-pressured, potentially unpredictable situations, on an almost daily basis, to achieve exceptional outputs, exceeding the highest of expectations, demonstrating and sharing expertise in the knowledge that every performance is being judged and contributes directly to the overall success of the business, then you probably don't need an elite team. And if you don't, then do consider what level of teamwork you do need, and what level of training is required to achieve it. To do anything more would be wasteful.

One other fascinating aspect of staff development and team management that appears to be unique to the restaurant world, and which is certainly a taken-for-granted part of their culture, is the way in which individuals are supported and, indeed, encouraged to move on to other establishments. Do you remember Gary Jones saying, 'One of my guys is moving on after six years with me. I've talked to him, making his future prospects clear. I've advised him where to go and work next. At this point in his career it is right for him to go away, gain some different experiences, and then realise that there is no place like home'?

This is the accepted, rather than the exceptional, approach. The senior chefs and managers are part of an international network through which staff can travel and learn. This cross-cultural/cross-business collaboration ensures the growth of talent throughout the industry. Each business hopes too, of course, that staff will not only learn more by experiencing other centres of excellence, but that they will eventually return bringing their learning with them. And, often, this is what happens. It is a classic example of a win-win situation and it makes one wonder why businesses in other industries don't adopt the practice.

Selfishness, experimentation and the value of holding a cat by its tail

Peter Senge, the man whose work helped to introduce and promote the value of the learning organisation, could have had our restaurants in his mind when he wrote, 'You cannot force commitment, what you can do... you nudge a little here, inspire a little there, and provide a role model. Your primary influence is the environment you create.'

Whatever differences exist between them, these three restaurant cultures are all built on the four interlocking powers of:

* Inspiration
* Leadership
* Learning
* Environments.

They all nudge, inspire and demonstrate. They understand how these four powers combine to create the two superpowers of context and identity. They know how environments influence, how they share messages about who *we* are, what *our* purpose is, and how *we* currently achieve it. They appreciate how environments which, we must remember, include systems as well as tangible structures and design, not only speak volumes about the realities of the culture, but also play a crucial role in reinforcing it. Michael Caines's admission that one of his primary skills was 'seeing space and turning it into a successful business reality,' reflects his understanding that environment does not just contain the context; in one important sense it *is* the context and it needs, therefore, to be managed to the highest degree.

The restaurants' commitment to constant learning and improvement and their willingness to be creative, to experiment and experience, reflects what might be thought of as a proper selfishness. By this, I mean a selfish pursuit of their own development in order to be able to serve their guests better. Such is the importance of learning in these organisations that it seems reasonable to suggest that a person's or a team's level of passion and commitment to the corporate cause can be measured by their desire to know more and to become better. Plato wrote that 'all learning has an emotional base.' Perhaps any truth in that assertion – and I witnessed much to support it during my time at the restaurants – derives from the fact that the desire to learn grows out of the passion that precedes it. Simply, if we care enough to need to be great at something, we care enough to make learning the cornerstone of our development.

From my observations, experimentation is a valued part of the restaurants' learning process. It is encouraged if not expected. These are all places in which learning is achieved by doing as well as by reflecting on the results achieved; in which questioning is as important as performing to the required standards. Indeed, their examples remind us that the ability to ask questions that lead to new insights that, in turn, lead to tangible improvements, is vital if high quality is to be maintained.

Experimentation is not without risk, however, although to these people it is a risk that is acknowledged and accepted rather than shied away from. Mark Twain's observation that 'if you hold a cat by the tail you learn things you cannot learn any other way', reminds us of both the value and the challenge of learning through experience and experimentation. In these restaurants, learning from personal experience is balanced by ensuring that staff learn also from the experience of others. Gary Jones's awareness of, and pride in, his role as a mentor is an attitude matched by managers throughout the three restaurants. And, in reverse, these senior managers also encourage and value input, ideas and questions from even the newest and least experienced members of their team. The view, taken by all of the senior managers, is that the naivety associated with inexperience can sometimes serve as a creative catalyst, spurring observations and leading to changes that might have been missed by those accustomed to the status quo or the accepted wisdom. Sometimes a little knowledge might be a dangerous thing; sometimes, though, if used correctly it seems that it can play a significant role in the creative and, therefore, the learning process.

One other noticeable aspect of their approach was the emphasis placed on ownership and personal responsibility. D. Blocher wrote, 'Learning is not a spectator sport.' I can report with certainty that there are no spectators within any of the teams I studied. Individuals have no option but to accept their part in the outcomes they create. Success is congratulated, celebrated or rewarded according to the nature and value of the result. Mistakes are owned just as completely, and not only by the person or people directly responsible. As I revealed in the stories, managers take ownership for the performance of their team and the individual members within it. The aim is to avoid mistakes if at all possible, however if they occur they become a new source of learning, and part of that learning is to take ownership of it. For this to be a positive and developmental experience, managers have to know how to delegate responsibly and appropriately and all involved need a high level of emotional intelligence.

Delegation is a potentially challenging necessity. It is necessary because, quite simply, there is usually too much work, and too much variety of work, for one person to be able to do it all within the time frame set and to the required standard. It can be challenging for three reasons:

1) Tasks need to be matched to individual expertise
2) Managers need to be willing to hand over the reins to others
3) Managers need to know how best to control each situation.

The successful matching of tasks to individuals is dependent upon the quality and appropriateness of the staff base, which takes us back inevitably to the importance of recruitment and selection. However, even if the best possible teams are in place, the challenge to know who to select and why still remains. Managers have to be clear about their reasons for delegation and the desired quality of outcome. In the restaurants I experienced managers delegating tasks for a variety of purposes and with a variety of different levels of control. Sometimes delegation was a part of training. Its purpose was to help develop an individual's skill and experience and the level of control was obvious and constant. Sometimes, particularly when only the very best result was acceptable, tasks were delegated to the most skilled and control, whilst present, was less obvious. Whatever the purpose, delegation only works well when managers are comfortable with the process, willing to share, and are cognisant of the fact that they are delegating authority and not responsibility – that ultimately and always the buck stops with them.

Managers in all three restaurants demonstrated this attitude with apparent ease. Perhaps the hierarchical structure of the businesses makes it easy and obvious for delegation to be so readily accepted? Perhaps it is because learning is such a constant presence and delegation such an important part of that? Or perhaps it is because you cannot share a congruent corporate identity through the work and behaviours of a minority of staff? Everyone, therefore, needs to be able to contribute to the deliberate sharing of who *we* are and that cannot be done unless managers delegate.

Whatever the reason, or combination of reasons, the ability to manage negative emotions is paramount. To be able to own a mistake, to accept responsibility for it in front of your peers, and then help identify and share the learning that comes from it, requires – if not control of a range of emotions – then at least a willingness to experience them in pursuit of growth. To work in these establishments is to accept emotional as well as physical pressure. It is present whenever Mourad challenges his team, or Diego has a private conversation with a member of staff showing what Frédéric Poulette calls his 'other face', or when Damien Bastiat asks after a successful twelve months, 'How do we do better this year?'

A high level of emotional control is needed not only to manage the discipline and rigour inherent in the pursuit of excellence, but also when managing guests. The unpredictability identified previously means that staff have to be alert to changes in attitude and able to manage their own responses. Again, it is expected that senior managers are better equipped to control their emotional reactions and, therefore, any awkwardness that might arise. Everyone also has to manage guests' delight, which is a far more commonplace experience, and one that brings with it its own challenges. Frequent success can dull the appetite for the hard work that underpins improvement; it can encourage a relaxing of attitude, an expectation that everything will go well just because it usually does. If achieving excellence is demanding, maintaining or improving upon it is even more so. Emotional intelligence in this regard means being able to start afresh each day, to believe genuinely that there is only one chance ever to get it right. To have a chance of doing that, everyone has to share the same beliefs, attitudes and perceptions and demonstrate them as they work together.

These day-to-day, minute-by-minute interactions are the details that make up the big picture, that reveal and share the identity of each place. The key is to ensure that these internal communications and experiences match those that are shared externally.

Being yourself: identity and integrity hand in hand

On a basic level it would seem that the three restaurants take a very different approach to communicating themselves to the outside world. For example, there is a discreet Marketing department in operation at Le Manoir, none such at The Waterside, whilst Gidleigh Park's external communication benefits from being part of Andrew Brownsword's hotel chain. The important commonality, though, is the congruency that exists between their external promise and the internal experience, between their portrayed identity and their everyday reality.

It is this synergy between who the restaurants claim to be – their professed public identity – and how they perform on a daily basis that marks them out. Kay Stepkin suggested that, 'Integrity means not violating one's own identity.' According to this definition, the restaurants come as close to demonstrating integrity as any business can be expected to. Importantly, if integrity is the consequence of congruent communications that stem from, and reflect, a clear sense of identity, there can be neither integrity nor great communications until or unless personal identity has been established.

Too often, I would suggest, corporate communications lack this foundation and this synergy. For many, communication is limited to marketing and PR. It is seen as the prerogative and responsibility of these specific departments. It is measured by the quality of the media they produce rather than everyone's commitment to 'walking the talk'. Too often, there exists a significant gap between what businesses say about themselves and how they actually operate. Not surprisingly customers disappear in that gap and are lost forever. The restaurants work consistently to limit that communication gap.[1] They understand that congruency is ultimately the result of integrated activities, the bringing together of every part of the business working in a coordinated manner towards the shared vision, and that the most influential communication is more a matter of great storytelling than it is the sharing of facts and figures.

Lila Swell wrote, 'Identity and success go hand in hand. Many people sacrifice their identities by not doing what they really want to. And that's why they're not successful.' Our restaurants are successful. Their success not only grows out of the clarity of their identity, it also promotes it. This is the double benefit that comes from communicating and demonstrating an identity and not just a product or service and the associated needs it satisfies.

Corporate identity, though, like passion, has to be found and developed. It is as much a result of the creative process as systems and architecture. It is a consequence of leadership decisions and managerial actions. It has to be developed fully and then communicated clearly so that everyone recognises its value, understands its uniqueness, and wants to engage with it.

Summary

The learning points in this chapter are:

1) Self-understanding underpins the development of a corporate identity which precedes the creation of the brand
2) Recruit staff who share your values and beliefs; who will represent your identity congruently
3) Invest in their development

---

1 If you want to know more about the communication gap and how to manage it, my next book *Closing the Communication Gap* will be published by Kogan Page in 2013.

4) Determine the level of team (or group) work needed in each department and create only the required level
5) Ensure that leaders are role models, that learning occurs both informally and formally, and that individuals and/or teams accept ownership
6) Respect the power of environments and create and manage accordingly
7) Integrate all aspects of internal and external communications.

One other point to remember: a congruent identity can include – even depend upon – a mixture of apparent opposites; getting this mixture right and knowing which to prioritise is an essential part of the leader's role. Raymond Blanc reflected this when he said:

'...the ideal runs separately and yet together with the commercial, but never the commercial first.'

Ingredient No. 3

Identify all the ways your location influences your business and then manage these positively

'There's a heaven for everybody. Only its location is different.'

Mariana Fulger

This ingredient comprises:
• The relationship between location, identity and cause; the place as an essential character
• The paradox of standing out whilst fitting in
• The nature and application of the Perimeter Principle
• The relationship between location, perception and imagination.

Standing firm, effective occupation and knowing the customer's place

The oft-quoted advice that the three most important factors in buying a home are 'location, location, location' is as relevant for businesses as it is for homeowners. The reason why this element is included as Ingredient No. 3 and not Nos. 1, 2 and 3 is that you cannot choose your business location until you have the first two ingredients ready for the mix. Of the many insights I gained during my study, the influence of location on so many aspects of each business was one of the most significant and informative.

For that reason the importance of location became a central feature in each story. I found myself unintentionally drawn to thinking of each place as a unique character in its own right. I became fascinated by the nature of the relationships that existed between the location and the people who either worked there or visited. Over time I came to appreciate that the success of these restaurants was not simply a result of how staff behaved on a short- or long-term basis, that they are not enormously popular just because of the quality of their food or customer service, or because of the significance of their histories or the appropriateness of their strategic planning. Their success is also due in no small measure to their location, and I mean that in its most complete sense. When I talk about the location of these businesses I am referring to their geographical setting, their outdoor spaces, their buildings and décor, and their virtual presence on the worldwide web. Abraham Lincoln urged, 'Be sure to put your feet in the right place, then stand firm.' The founders and leaders of our three restaurants have done just that. By doing so they have provided us with some more invaluable lessons about how to achieve and maintain business success.

Two of our stories, those about Le Manoir and The Waterside, began with the finding of the right location. In both cases the founder of each business recognised the potential of the place and had to work to create his vision. It was a vision not only about what the place would look like, but also how it would operate and what it would represent. Inevitably, both Raymond Blanc and Michel Roux Snr impressed their personalities and values into the location, using the space to make statements about their roots, their intentions and their appreciation of the place they had just made home. At Gidleigh Park we see a different, although equally committed, relationship between people and place. Andrew Brownsword writes his love affair with Gidleigh and his role as custodian. The work he commissioned to develop the building and the grounds was done with at least one eye fixed firmly on the past. It offers the very best of modern comfort in a style that is in keeping – perhaps it would be more accurate to say in *admiration* – of the way things were. Here it is easy to imagine that the custodian, rather than the businessman, led the change.

This leads to one of those unexpected and interesting observations about the power of location on those who own it: in all three examples the place exerts a powerful influence on those who created it. Damien Bastiat's description of Gidleigh Park as a 'fine old lady' is perhaps the most obvious example, although we can remember, too, Andrew Foulkes's long-term desire to work there. We can think of Raymond Blanc's passion for both the house and the gardens at Le Manoir, and his willingness to spend extremely large sums of money just to improve one room. We can appreciate how the apparent simplicity of The Waterside, the smallest of our locations, is created to remind everyone that this is home to a dynasty and a legacy; only this and the river's timeless flow.

It has been fascinating to watch these places – which have been, at the very least, shaped and developed, managed and cared for by individuals and teams – become even more important than those people. Each location has a unique *feel* about it that I attempted to describe in the stories. I believe this feeling is deliberately created through the mixture of elements I am going to talk about in this chapter. It is the result of the deliberate management of each layer, or perimeter, of the business and the interactions between them. It is the consequence of the behaviours of staff, the design of buildings and grounds, the relationship the place shares with its neighbours, the expectations of guests, and that very precise sense of identity.

To say that these locations are fit for purpose, would be both completely accurate and somehow simplistic. They are, like all aspects of these businesses, developed and managed with great attention to detail and precision. Indeed, the deliberateness that, one can argue, is at the very heart of the restaurants' business success, is most obvious through their location management. Unless a visit to the kitchen is on the agenda, guests rarely see the incredibly focused and demanding work that consumes the chefs and, equally, each front of house team is keen to be seen and heard only when the situation warrants it. However, the buildings and grounds, the website and other aspects of the virtual perimeter are quite literally staring us in the face. And they share a story if we choose to look and listen.

It is through the management of the location that these business leaders and their staff show us most obviously who they are, what they offer, and how they want to be perceived and experienced. The lavender path at Le Manoir is both a greeting and a message from Raymond Blanc, summarising many of his values and preparing you for more. The sign en route to Gidleigh Park telling to us 'Take heart' both welcomes and encourages in a way designed to create a positive shift in the traveller's mindset. The photos of the Roux dynasty hanging in the reception at The Waterside Inn show a loving family and friends who also happen to be some of the world's most influential chefs.

William James wrote, 'Knowledge about life is one thing; effective occupation of a place in life with its dynamic currents passing through your being is another.' The individuals who lead and manage these locations demonstrate this most effective of occupations; there is a dynamic current running through both the people and the places. Somehow they have managed to create a place that best reflects them. Their appreciation that location is a most significant form of communication, combined with their creative abilities and their strategic and tactical awareness, has led to the establishment of establishments that are carefully designed, presented and managed; establishments which not only reflect the personalities of those in charge but which have also, over time, developed a character and a significance of their own.

Of course, the individual feel of each place does not exist without people to experience it. We have to acknowledge, therefore, our role in creating and/or defining just precisely what it is. The learning point is that our three locations are managed quite deliberately to create a desired effect on both staff and guests. After all, whether locations are managed carefully or not, they are inevitably powerful mediums of communication. The logic, therefore, would be to have a clear desired end outcome and to assume responsibility for achieving it. The people I studied knew that their location played a crucial role in determining the guests' experience, and the guests' perspective is always firmly in their minds.

There is always a risk that managers and staff become accustomed to regarding and experiencing the location in which they work from their own perspective – from the inside looking out. Guests, however, have the opposite experience: they engage with every business from the outside looking in. When staff forget this, their ability to manage their location effectively diminishes. The American writer Orison Swett Marden said, 'The golden rule for every businessman is this: "Put yourself in your customers' shoes."' With regard to location, that begins by assuming the outside-in perspective and by then tracking it through every aspect of the guest's experience. We will return to this point later; for now, though, suffice to say that the senior managers in each of our three locations are acutely aware of the need to wear someone else's footwear when seeking to influence.

They are all also aware of the power that a name can have, of how people quickly learn to associate experiences and emotions with it. Interestingly, too, the names of the restaurants are often abbreviated when people refer to them. Those who know Gidleigh Park – staff, guests and the local population – call her simply 'Gidleigh'; The House for All Seasons becomes 'Le Manoir'; and the 'Inn' is usually left out by people talking about 'The Waterside'. By abbreviating a name we demonstrate at least an understanding of the subject and, often, an intimacy. Names that encourage an easy abbreviation encourage this association, and beyond that they offer an implied message about the power of their brand: that they are so well known, so strong in the marketplace, that just the abbreviated version is now enough to ensure recognition.

Our restaurants remind us that, one way or the other, location is an essential character in the story and the experience of a business. It is a character that, when utilised to its best, motivates staff and furthers the sense of belonging. It influences guests positively, reveals corporate identity and cause, and is a central component of communication and marketing. I can't help but wonder how many of these positive features are lost – and what negative features inadvertently take their place – when the management of location is not prioritised?

First-rate originality

The apparent paradox that each restaurant has had to address is how to establish their own unique world that also fits in with their surroundings. It is a potential challenge because they have each set out to create what we can think of as first-rate originality whilst simultaneously becoming an accepted and valued part of the local environment and community. Somehow standing-out and fitting-in have to be combined. The way of doing this might become more obvious if we accept Marianne Moore's view that originality is a 'by-product of sincerity.'

The sincerity that runs through these three businesses is a consequence of their commitment to their cause, vision and values. Their originality is based on the clarity of their identity. Their longevity is dependent in part on their ability to sustain meaningful relationships with all key stakeholders. Throughout my time at the restaurants I saw myriad examples of how they each relate to, and with, those around them and how they have integrated themselves into their location.

The music festivals and Christmas carol services held at the church next door to Le Manoir are a traditional part of The House's yearly calendar and form an obvious connection between the business and the community. At The Waterside the river is both a source of relaxation and a means of transport, connecting the restaurant with other local businesses and homes; guests can choose to sail there or they can be collected in The Waterside's boat if they do not have access to their own. Alain Roux's most famous culinary neighbour, Heston Blumenthal, is based only a few hundred metres from The World at the End of the Road and the two share a mutual, cooperative respect rather than operating purely as competitors. In Devon,

Gidleigh's relationship with the moor and nearby communities is well established. It is helped by the fact that Michael Caines is a local boy who does much to promote his home region.

This creation of networks and ongoing interaction with local life helps to strengthen and further the corporate identity of each restaurant. It reinforces the point that a business, just like a person, can have a distinct personality and focus without creating distance from those around them. Indeed, each restaurant demonstrates how you can have your own identity, fit in with your immediate surroundings and community and also show your connections with places much further afield and with times that have passed, and do this all in a seemingly effortless manner. All three restaurants are successful places in their own right and yet make clear that they are also a part of something bigger. They are connected to their past, and *belong* within their location, and this sense of belonging has not happened by accident. It has been managed, just like every other part of their enterprise.

Interestingly, they have all managed to achieve this integration whilst building their own, individual world in microcosm – and each does feel like an individual world. Each is home to a specific set of promises, expectations, social norms and experiences. Each has its own history and its own style. Each has its own borders that you have to cross to gain entry. These might not be obvious and they are certainly all welcoming in nature, however there are specific demarcation points that assist the visitors in leaving their usual reality behind. These unique worlds are the breeding ground for the cause. However much each business is entwined within its location, each cause is more firmly embedded within the distinct business world that has been developed both to contain and to grow it. The great singer and entertainer Judy Garland advised, 'Always be a first-rate version of yourself, instead of a second-rate version of somebody else.' Arguably the best way to achieve this is to create a world that reveals your – and only your – identity and purpose.

To make these worlds vibrant and appealing they need to

be populated, developed and enriched by individuals with the learning, the life experiences and the dreams to be able to take responsibility for their growth and sustainability. They need to be people who love the actual place as much as they do its purpose, people who cannot emotionally distinguish their cause from their location. In the first instance these are the leaders and their 'field marshals'. Beyond that, each business works to develop this same emotional bond within their staff and/or to attract those who already feel it.

One common aspect of these three different worlds is the way they have very carefully ensured, and manage, a connection between the external and the internal facets of their space. In each place the natural world impacts upon and, in some way or another, influences within the buildings. At Le Manoir, for example, bedroom names and designs reflect external influences; guests can enjoy organised garden tours, which serve also to emphasise the importance of the relationship between the potager and the kitchen. At The Waterside the patio doors that form the river-facing wall of the restaurant are opened whenever the weather allows it to let nature merge with the measured management of the dining experience. And at Gidleigh the open fires, the flowers, the view down the valley, the wellingtons in the entrance and the availability of planned walks on the moor, all combine to reinforce the natural connection. Scott Andrews's observation that when diners leave most restaurants they walk out onto a city street is indicative of the awareness these managers have of how best to mix with, and take advantage of, the unique nature of their locations. It is an indication, too, of the various decisions they have all made about how much they should fit in with their location and how much they should stand out.

The Perimeter Principle © and the great art

They stand out, as I have already suggested, because of the deliberate and detailed ways they consistently demonstrate their identity. It is their understanding of what I call the Perimeter Principle that enables them to do this.

The Perimeter Principle is a useful and practical model and approach that I developed many years ago when working as a consultant and management trainer. The model is simply a series of concentric circles representing the number of perimeters a specific business has. A perimeter is any virtual or physical boundary that a customer, or potential customer, can encounter when engaging with the organisation.

In most cases the first perimeter is a virtual one, removed from the actual premises and the actual experience of the specific product or service. It can include a website, marketing materials, phone calls, letters, emails and signage. It is intended to bring customers and the business together, to make sales happen as positively and easily as possible, and/or to manage complaints or problems.[1] The next perimeter is often the entrance to the site and car parking facilities. The third is usually the entrance to the building and reception. And so it progresses through whatever different layers of the business the customer can experience.

The model is used to identify every interaction that can occur between customers (or suppliers) and the organisation. These interactions can be with staff, with automated systems, or just the experience of route ways. The aim is to determine the quality of these interactions, to measure them against the purported identity and values of the business, to check for congruency in the sharing of verbal and non-verbal messages, and to look for consistency in behaviours, timings and delivery. When applying the model it is necessary to:

1) Use it to evaluate the visitors' outward journey, their experiences when *leaving* the business, as well as their inward journey on arrival

2) Use it to evaluate the interactions that occur *between* each perimeter, as visitors move through the business environment.

---

1 Obviously this is the only perimeter for those involved solely in e-commerce.

The Perimeter Principle is an effective way of assessing every individual aspect of a business and, more importantly, gauging the synergy throughout.

I am certain that none of the managers in the restaurants had either heard of this model or deliberately created their own version. I was fascinated, therefore, to observe that they were all acutely aware of a) what each of their perimeters was, b) the need to manage each fully, c) the value of managing the transition from one perimeter to another and d) the importance of ensuring a great ending.

In each case this appeared to be done instinctively, as if it were just the obvious way to manage the guest experience, synchronise all communications, and maintain overall standards. No one talked to me about 'perimeters' or managing visitor interactions or experiences between them, however the systems in place and attitudes of staff meant that this attention to detail and 'joined-up' behaviour was a part of the everyday operation of each restaurant. Given that their locations and identities are very different, each place goes about it differently. With one exception, the examples I am going to offer provide insights only into some aspects of each restaurant's approach and methods to managing the first perimeters.

Due to its unique location, those booked to visit Gidleigh Park receive specific directions telling them how best to reach the house. This is not only a useful and practical support, it also serves to prepare first-time guests for the single-track road that links Gidleigh to the outside world, and makes clear the peaceful isolation it offers. The 'Take heart' sign can be viewed as the Gidleigh culture stretching out beyond its obvious boundaries, offering encouragement and providing a link between what lies ahead and what has been left behind. The key to its value is in the language used, not just its positioning. The grounds at Gidleigh are managed such that a wonderful view of the property and the gardens open up suddenly when the final bend has been turned; there is at once a revealing and a sense of arrival that, one imagines, makes many guests sigh with both relief and delight at the sight of the house standing centre stage in its carefully presented environment.

Guests drive round to the back of the house to park. Views from the car park look over the herb garden and grounds and down the valley. Guests' arrival is observed and a member of staff is waiting to greet them at the house. Again, signage is used to reinforce the nature of the place and support the human greeting. The 'Once upon a time' carving above the front door is a clear statement of intent and style. The wellingtons and old pictures of the house that are in the entrance connect Gidleigh both to the moor and to its past – two essential components of its character. Inside, the lack of a reception desk, coupled with the fire, flowers and comfortable seating, is intended to make guests feel at home rather than in a hotel; it speaks of a lack of unnecessary formality and of a desire to provide comfort and quality in a manner that encourages everyone simply to relax.

Before arriving at Le Manoir brown, tourist road signs point the way. Apart from making life easy for drivers en route, they also emphasise the prestigious and popular nature of the destination. The message is: This is an important part of our community that many people visit; we recognise this and want to help you on your way. The signs are an apparently simple and yet significant indication of how successful Raymond Blanc has been at simultaneously both fitting in and standing out.

Le Manoir is just visible from the main road for those who are looking. The comparative peace and tranquillity of the village road leading to The House marks a sudden shift in attitude and state. Within a few hundred metres the entrance, elegant and simple, draws you in and the drive leads to the car park, which offers views of The House and the grounds. A small, discreet summerhouse accommodates staff waiting to welcome new arrivals. Umbrellas are provided if it is raining. The walk from the car park is along the lavender path. With aspects of Provence on either side, a view of the gardens to their right and a classic English country house ahead of them, guests walk away from their car and ever deeper into the world of RB. The experience is enhanced by greetings from every member of staff who happens to pass by.

Gidleigh Park and Le Manoir both use their extensive space to create layers of transition, to invite guests to move physically and emotionally away from their everyday routine and towards and into the carefully planned and managed experience that awaits them. They appreciate that travel and transition are an essential part of people's holiday experience and if they are to create a luxurious, albeit usually brief, equivalent, if they are to build a sense of expectation and excitement and make sure that guests feel distanced from their norm, they have to let them pass through several layers of experience. Sequencing is as important in this regard as it is in storytelling. Indeed, as I have already suggested, in one sense this is a form of storytelling and when there is physical space available, its role is a significant one. When there isn't such space, people have to create the layers instead.

At The Waterside, where space is at a premium, this is precisely what happens. The riverside location is undeniably relaxing, however it can only be reached by walking briefly through the buildings. Consequently, the grand beginning at The Waterside – which, like all grand beginnings, requires the feeling of a journey travelled, a significant sense of arrival, a greeting (or greetings) and an entrance (or entrances) – is dependent solely upon the skill and teamwork of the staff. When grounds and gardens cannot be structured to add their effect, the responsibility for starting the guests' experience well, for turning their arrival into an event that clearly marks their admission into a new, distinct world, lies with the people who meet and greet them.

On one level the sense of arrival at The Waterside is emphasised by the fact that the restaurant is quite literally at the end of the road: there is nowhere else to go without going swimming. The most significant element, though, is the greeting of Oliver, the doorman waiting to welcome you, park your car and, most importantly, begin the process of immersing you in the place rather than the river.

Once inside the building two things combine to create and reinforce this immersion. The more obvious of these is the way and frequency with which members of staff greet guests as they are led inwards. The other, equally powerful influencer is the culture, the absolutely accepted way of behaving, the type of congruent difference we experience whenever we visit a new place that is so steeped in its own history, values and norms that those who live there not only take it for granted, they cannot imagine living a different way. Here, though, it is a deliberate process enacted to demonstrate and welcome guests into a new world in as few paces as possible.

At The Waterside, as well as at Gidleigh and Le Manoir, the quality of the welcome has to be first-rate and then has to be surpassed by what follows. And, given that the very last memory people will take away with them is the nature of their departure, the ending has to be as personal and professional as everything that has gone before. Henry Wadsworth Longfellow wrote, 'Great is the art of beginning, but greater is the art of ending.' In every story the ending has to be worthy of what precedes it. If it is not, the result is always and only disappointment. The same is true for every customer-business interaction. Brilliant customer service should not end once money has been transferred. Indeed, I would argue that the quality of customer service is best measured when the organisation has no immediate or short-term gain to be made through the current communication. Few people want to be simply sold to; most want to be engaged with. And often that engagement can continue for as long as the business chooses – if they manage the communication and the customer experience well.

In all three restaurants attention is paid to the endings, to the guests' outward journeys. The aim is for them to leave as well as they arrived, with the added bonus of great memories to keep. The restaurants practise and demonstrate the art of the great ending. They know that the better you manage your perimeters and what happens betwixt and between, the more your reputation stretches out into your immediate location and beyond.

Location, perception and imagination

It is easy to think that creativity in these restaurants starts and ends in the kitchen. The shared search for continual improvement, however, means that this is not the case; all managers and their teams look for creative solutions. And they have very obvious examples to follow because each place began, of course, in the imagination of highly creative and committed individuals. The businesses we can now experience and the ways they interact within their geographical location are the result of imagination made real and exercised continually. Ursula K. LeGuin wrote, 'It is above all by the imagination that we achieve perception and compassion and hope.'

The senior managers work hard to ensure that their perception of the environment is never blinkered, and to this end they do everything they can to prevent their imagination becoming a prisoner of their own routines. Systems and routines are an inevitable and essential part of organisational life. Used well they can create effectiveness and efficiency, demonstrate ownership and enhance the customer experience. The risk, though, is that even necessary repetition can dull perception and limit imagination. We have seen examples of how those in the restaurants seek to combat this. Diego varies his entrance to The Waterside each day; he admits to creating problems for his staff to resolve just to keep them alert. Philip Newman-Hall makes a point of putting himself in the guest's position, staying overnight and experiencing Le Manoir from the outside-in perspective. For Michael Caines, the fact that he works away from Gidleigh for several days each week means that he can bring a fresh perspective with him every time he returns.

Location also fires the imagination and, therefore, the expectation of guests. Images shared through various media begin this process and it is important to note that these images are supported in no small way by the choice of language that accompanies them. Words and phrases trigger responses in the human brain. They spark associations, lead us to conclusions, incite our emotions. An awareness of the location we are planning to visit, where it is situated, the way it looks and how it is described, combine to create a mixture of feelings that might be best summarised as those of hopefulness. We so hope that it will really be as good as it looks, that we will feel great being there, that it is worth the commitment we, as customers, are making.

The relationship between location, perception and imagination is, then, a most powerful one. It has to be managed positively on a day-to-day basis by the professionals involved, knowing that it is also what draws their guests towards them in the first instance. Location, perception and imagination are three of the key elements that fuse together to establish reputation. Reviews, word-of-mouth reports, and all other forms of feedback and information-sharing serve only to stir perception and imagination. Location is the almost taken for granted, often ignored, influencer of reputation. As guests we tend to report on the quality of customer service and/or the products, on the nature of the human interaction and the qualities and skills of the professionals we encounter. However, location and all that entails creates the context, the boundaries, the atmosphere, within which it all happens. The location of the business, the way its perimeters are created and managed, the relationships built between the business and its neighbours, how it fits into the wider environment and how it stands out, tell us more about the people and the ambitions of the place than arguably anything else.

The German poet and author Christian Morganstern wrote, 'Home is not where you live, but where they understand you.' These restaurants are home to the people who have created and continue to manage them and to the ideals that continue to drive them. To understand these, simply study their location. It speaks volumes.

Summary

The learning points in this chapter are:

1. Location includes geographical setting, outdoor spaces, buildings and décor, and any virtual presence

2. Location is a powerful communicator, influencing those who work there as well as all visitors
3. Location needs to be selected, developed, maintained and managed with absolute deliberateness
4. Identity and purpose are revealed through location management
5. A balance needs to be achieved between fitting in and standing out
6. The Perimeter Principle is a model and approach that enables management of all aspects of the location, communication and the guests' experience
7. Experience and understand the guests' perception of your location; use this to create improvements.

One other point to remember: although the successful daily management of location is dependent upon the use of systems and routines, creativity and imagination are essential to its development and continual success. As Michael Caines said:

'Really creative people… are not comfortable with routine. They are restless. This is the difference between those who create and innovate and those who follow.'

Ingredient No. 4

Learn everything you can about your customers and then use this to guide all your behaviours

'When the customer comes first, the customer will last.'

Robert Half

This ingredient comprises:
- Customer analysis and understanding
- The relationship between understanding and action
- Flexible communication styles and methods
- Information management; storing, updating and sharing information in an appropriate and timely manner.

The noblest pleasure and an elegant match

This ingredient is a vital part of the mix because, in simplest terms, customers pay the wages and the bills. It is an ingredient that is well understood and used by all three restaurants. Yet, interestingly, it is clear that customer analysis and the understanding gathered from that, and the many ways that understanding is then applied, grows out of the desire to serve guests rather than the business need to keep the paymasters happy.

The people I studied were, as I have already discussed, driven by an emotional need to serve and to provide, rather than just to be financially successful. They are great examples of the principle that the best way to create and maintain a successful business is to begin by ensuring that your work is based on your passion and then to apply great business principles and practices to it.

One of the messages that all three restaurants shared loud and clear is this: to be brilliant, indeed, just to strive for brilliance, requires enormous commitment and dedication; to make these sacrifices purely for financial gain, to work so hard without the emotional compulsion associated with a cause, without truly caring about – and believing in – the purpose of your business is, in some ways at least, to live a hollow existence. When Raymond Blanc explains, 'The ideal and the commercial necessity are opposites. They coexist together, but they repel each other very often. I learnt that many years ago because I was a raging idealist. I would only think of beauty and never the cost. I have done it, suffered from it, made my mistakes.' And when Diego Masciaga describes the 'difficult chain', that is the relationship between quality, service and profit, we are hearing two men speaking about the inevitable clash when passion meets commercial necessity, when the desire to serve, which was – and remains – their primary motivation, is tempered against the need to do great business. All three stories introduce us to managers and leaders who are always having to balance heart and head, knowing when to quench emotional thirst with business logic. In all cases, though, heart came first and the business was, and continues to be, built around it.

The quality of the guests' experience, then, is crucial to the ongoing success of these businesses, and the quality of that experience is dependent upon more than just a desire to serve and the accompanying skill sets. It requires an understanding of guests and the ability to share that information as and when it is needed. Leonardo da Vinci wrote, 'The noblest pleasure is the joy of understanding.' It is, however, a pleasure that has to be earned through the rigours of analysis, and it has to have a purpose beyond just the pleasure of understanding. For the restaurants, as for most other businesses, that purpose is an enhanced customer experience leading to greater customer satisfaction. Actually it is not just customer satisfaction that the restaurants aim for, it is customer delight.

As a general rule there are nine basic steps in the customer analysis process. They are:

1) Identify your target market
2) Determine what you need to know about them
3) Determine and implement the best ways to gain this information
4) Analyse your results
5) Test to make sure that your analysis is accurate
6) Determine how this understanding will influence your products, services and environments
7) Ensure mechanisms for sharing this understanding with necessary others and/or for implementing required changes
8) Test to clarify that a common understanding has been reached and/or that changes have been implemented successfully
9) Get the timing right for all of the above.

Although the restaurants offer a high-end luxury product and experience, their target market extends beyond those who can afford to visit them regularly. They are all acutely aware that some guests visit at best very infrequently and some only once to celebrate the most special of occasions. They are all, therefore, keen to determine the guests' reasons for visiting, any special requirements they might have and how these might best be served during their stay.

At Le Manoir, for example, those staff responsible for managing telephone bookings not only have to achieve high standards of communication and information-sharing, they also have to be skilled at gathering a wide range of essential information. No matter how a business seeks to understand its customers, at the heart of the process is the ability to ask really good questions and then to listen really carefully to the answers.

It is a process, I would suggest, that is based on curiosity and respect. It is what we might think of as a headline activity created by a heartfelt need. That need, of course, is the cause.

For people with a desire to serve there is an obvious logic connected to the emotion that states:

'The more I understand about you, why you are visiting us, the nature of your current relationship with us, what you are expecting, what specific needs you have and what memories you hope to take away with you, the more chance I have of exceeding your expectations.'

We will talk about expectation management in the next chapter. For now, we will remind ourselves that questions can be asked for many reasons and at different times during the customer relationship process. In our book *Campaign It!* Alan Barnard and I wrote the following about the nature and importance of asking great questions:

'When we are ready to begin questioning, we need then to be clear about the value and purpose of the questions we are going to ask. We need to determine why we are asking every question we do... Sometimes we ask questions because we need to learn more. In these situations our questions are, initially at least, of value to us rather than others. Either way, we need to preface all the research we do by answering the question:

'Whom are we asking this question for?'

Whatever the purpose, questions are most valuable when formed in the language of those being questioned. For responses to be informative and reliable questions have to be understood as intended. To create the best possible chance of this happening they need to be asked using the other person's preferred language patterns and style and be framed within their life experience, not that of the questioner.

Nine useful questions to ask yourself before you question another are:

• Do I need to ask a question *now*?
• What am I currently unaware of in this situation?
• What assumptions are driving my behaviour?
• What is the most useful question I can ask now?

- What is the best way to frame and ask the question?
- What size of information do I need to gather?
- What kind of information do I need to gather?
- What kind of state do I wish the other person to induce in him/herself by answering my question?
- How does this question help move us closer to the desired end-outcome?

Often, of course, we will need to ask a series of questions. The order in which our questions are sequenced plays an important role in determining the level of focus and engagement of those being questioned and, consequently, the value of their responses. Sequencing gives the interviewees time to warm up to both the task and the topic and helps create within them the most useful emotional state. Throughout the discussion it is essential that we develop and pursue only the most fruitful lines of enquiry, whilst recognising, questioning and thus clarifying any ambiguities in the interviewee's responses.'

Obviously, in the restaurants the first round of questioning occurs before the guest arrives, when enquiries and a booking are being made. At this point questions tend to be framed to identify the reason for the visit, the duration, the number of guests, and any dining or accommodation requirements. It is information designed to enable planning and preparation. Questions might be asked at other times during the interaction for other reasons. These can be of a tactical nature, for example during the immediacy of service to determine how guests are responding to specifics, and/or of a more strategic nature to gain insights into how guests are relating to the overall nature of their experience. Sometimes a question about a specific detail can become the starting point for a strategic shift. For this to happen, though, the person responsible for the question needs to be able to recognise the value of the answer in a wider context and, importantly, then be willing to explore it further.

The most obvious example of this within our stories was Raymond Blanc's very specific question to his guests about their preference for either duvets or blankets: one apparently very simple question relating to the guests' comfort that led to additional questions and eventually a brand new strategic plan. Raymond's innate curiosity and respect for his guests, coupled with his desire to be at the forefront of change, was highlighted when, as you might recall, he said, 'I spend so much time trying to understand our guests. And what is the biggest change going to be in five or ten years' time? Nutrition. There's no doubt about it. We are going to eat far better than we do now. And that means gastronomy will have to change. That means the offering, the way it is served, and what is being served... So that is what I do, I try to steer this place towards the truly important changes in the lifestyle of our guests.'

I remind you of this simply because it is a great example of how successful business leaders are driven by the need to understand:

a) The most important aspects of their guests', or potential guests', current experiences and expectations
b) How these are most likely to change in the near future.

Curiosity can be thought of as the antidote to the creeping apathy easily spawned by routine and repetition. Curiosity is the attitude from which questions most easily grow. It challenges existing norms in the most positive of ways. Curiosity just wants to know why we are doing it like this and if we could do it better. It asks, 'What is it that we need to know that we currently don't and, once we do know this, what are we going to do about it?' Curiosity is the friend of those seeking to achieve and maintain excellence. Like any good friend, it can be challenging at times.

Alain Roux made brief reference to the difficulty of maintaining excellence during my time at The Waterside. Although, of course, he did it in his own very quiet way, when he said, 'Every day, every table, every individual guest, we have to perform to the highest standard... It is exciting. It is a pressure. It is part of the job. It is very difficult to get to the top, but to stay there is the hardest.'

Curiosity can also dare us to change and, sooner or later, it introduces its best friend, Creativity. Business leaders cannot be curious for its own sake; there has to be a purpose and that is always, and simply, continued success in changing times. To be curious without having creative capability is to be a spectator. And as we have already established, learning – which, even at the most basic level, comes from curiosity – is not a spectator sport.

Let's take a moment to revisit Michael Caines's observation about the need for curiosity and creativity to wrap around identity, rather than replace it. He said, 'If you are truly creative, there is a constant striving. Durability and endurance are so important. I'm always benchmarking. You have constantly to re-evaluate what you are doing in the marketplace without losing your values. I don't believe our industry is so special, we can learn from many things in life, but I am always saying to myself, "That's not me, so how would I do it?"... When it comes down to you, your time and your calling, you have to believe that people will come to you because of your identity, your point of difference.'

Sometimes, though, questions are asked by guests rather than by staff, and they are not always questions related to the current interaction. In these situations, the ability to manage conversations about a wide range of possible topics is important. This is why Diego keeps up to date with current affairs. The question he is always asking himself is, 'What are our guests likely to want to talk about today?' For Diego, this is just another level of understanding that can be used to build a relationship with guests, lead to further insights and enhance the quality of service and the overall experience.

The process of learning about and understanding guests is a continual one that is prioritised by each of our three restaurants. It is particularly important during the build-up to and the immediacy of service. Information about who guests are, their reasons for visiting and any dietary requirements or special requests, is recorded and passed on to the restaurant manager. This is then shared during the staff briefings that take place in the final minutes before guests arrive. The aim is to make sure that individual staff members know the essential details about the people they are serving, and that this information directs their behaviours. For example, in the same restaurant during any one service there might be several tables at which guests are engaged in business meetings; at other tables couples might be sharing an anniversary or a birthday celebration; there might even be a marriage proposal taking place! And, then, there will be those people who have just come out for no reason other than to enjoy a great meal and great service. To a casual observer everyone is doing the same thing, and yet a deeper understanding reveals that all have different needs and, therefore, different measures of what will make a great experience.

These measures can only be met, or exceeded, if they are clearly identified and known by all involved. Although each restaurant has its own systems in operation during service, there is always scope for the flexibility needed to meet personal needs. Discreet observation is the key to recognising how guests are responding to their experience and managing them accordingly. The information gathered about guests prior to their arrival is used as the foundation upon which service is based; the information-gathering, however, continues for as long as guests are present. The aim is to be able to anticipate needs, to know when to engage in conversation and when not to, to be able to inform the kitchen if timings need to change, to maximise the enjoyment of guests and to make everything seem as effortless as possible.

This understanding of guests' needs and the constant sharing of information was, for me, one of the most impressive and unexpected revelations of my study. I had, somewhat naively, presumed that customer information would be limited to dietary requirements and any celebratory special requests. Instead, I watched restaurant managers prime their teams to provide a level of individual service that I was able to recognise only because they allowed me to observe them in the way that they observe their diners. Otherwise I would have missed the hidden-away details that combine to make their service exceptional.

I watched an elderly diner on an especially hot summer day being discreetly monitored for fluid intake and any signs of adverse reaction to the heat as he enjoyed his lunch. The observation was so difficult to spot, done with such subtlety, that perhaps only members of the SAS could have disguised it better, and through it all the service was delivered with a gentle respect that still marked him out as the head of his table.

I witnessed a restaurant manager asking his team if anyone knew whether a marriage proposal made prior to the start of dinner service had been accepted and, when it was clear that no one did, instructing the waitress serving at that table to look for an engagement ring as a matter of priority! It was important because the answer to the proposal was going to influence precisely how the staff behaved towards the couple; the nature of their performance being determined by the current state of that particular 'audience'.

And this is the point – the one made in different ways by the restaurant managers in all the businesses: service is a form of performance. Only it is an interactive performance, one in which the audience, the diners, play a crucial role. In the theatre, performers can speak the same lines or play the same music night after night. In these restaurants, improvisation is king. Although the setting and the essential goal remain the same, the route taken to achieve it, the nature of the interactions along the way, is open to change. It is influenced not only by the guests' reasons for being there, but also by how they might change during the experience. Service is a script that is only ever, at best, half-written before the 'show' begins. The rest is created in the moment during the dynamic interaction between guests, the environment and the staff.

On a personal note, I have been studying and teaching interpersonal communication for over three decades and I was intrigued to watch restaurant managers and their senior staff members especially work to create a very deliberate influence on their guests. One three-step approach to building rapport and then managing an interaction in a positive manner is often summarised as:

Match---Pace---Lead.

To match means to copy, or share, the other party's communication patterns and to engage with their current reality. The first step, then, is to match the person's verbal and body language along with other relevant factors such as their interests, intentions, values and even their emotional state. All of these can be identified by asking questions, observing behaviours and/or through background research.

The purpose of matching is to create a sense of likeness and rapport. Research shows that we are most susceptible to the influence of people we like, or who we perceive to be like us. When this level of rapport has been reached, it is tested and maintained. This is the pacing part of the process, building the relationship, ensuring that rapport is established, before taking the lead and directing the interaction towards your desired outcome.

Research also reveals that we are more willing to follow the lead of those we regard as experts in the context within which we are operating and/or those who have the authority that comes from being in a specific role. Simply put, if you can show that you understand the other person, or people, that you share at least some things in common, that you have an expertise that is of value to them and that you are willing to give them your attention, your potential to influence is high.

I watched aspects of this approach being applied in all three restaurants with significant effect. Diego Masciaga, Damien Bastiat and Mourad Ben Tefka all appreciate the perceived power of their role and associated status and, along with their staff, they use their understanding of guests to help them relate in ways that build the required level of rapport; they then direct the interaction in ways designed to best meet the guests' needs. Front of house teams also seek to influence guests' behaviour and the overall atmosphere within the restaurant through their own mannerisms. They walk at a speed intended to imply and encourage a sense of calmness. They talk to guests using the noise level they wish to encourage.

It was also interesting to observe how they controlled their behaviour when they were not directly interacting with guests; like actors who are on stage but not delivering lines they understood that they were still contributing to the overall performance, that they were creating an influence just by being present. And, when not interacting directly, they were able to continue looking and listening, to keep gathering feedback. As might be expected, the restaurant managers never stop doing this. Despite the demands of service they were all skilled at maintaining emotional control, capable of being in the moment and yet outside of it at the same time. Their role requires them to keep one eye on the totality of what is happening around them and the other on specific details. They are responsible for managing staff, guests and the interface with the kitchen team. To do this, they need to be able to identify, interpret, decide and then act swiftly and repeatedly, and they need to be able to do so with elegance.

One loop and endless different worlds

Whether Diego, Damien or Mourad and their protégés have ever heard of the OODA Loop developed by military strategist John Boyd is irrelevant. They all act according to its principles instinctively and successfully. The OODA Loop comprises the following four elements:
• Observe
• Orient
• Decide
• Act.

Boyd argued that success in combat and, by extension, any other form of challenging situation, is achieved by managing these four elements better and more swiftly than those around you.

Observation is the ability to see what is happening, to have awareness of the situation and to gather the information on which decisions will be based. This leads into orientation, which is the filtering and processing of this information so that an interpretation and conclusion can be reached. The challenge is to do so without letting personal bias get in the way. Personally, I wonder if even a Zen Master is genuinely capable of this. However the evidence from extensive research shows us that, with sufficient training and experience in a given context, individuals can interpret experiences accurately and surprisingly quickly, often intuitively, and then use this to decide what action to take. Making a decision is the third stage in the OODA Loop. As the fourth stage is Action, the Loop reminds us that to make a decision is to commit to behaviour with the intention of achieving a specific outcome.

It doesn't end there, though. These four elements are presented as a loop because this is a continual process. Once action has been taken, the results are observed and interpreted, the next decision is made and the next action applied. And so it goes on.

The key to success in applying the OODA Loop is to do so more swiftly and accurately than those around you and to be flexible in both your thinking and your responses. When Frédéric Poulette at The Waterside Inn says, 'Mr Diego is always one step ahead. I try to be one step ahead of everyone else, but he is always ahead of me,' he is talking about his manager's ability to observe, orient, decide and act faster and more accurately than those around him and, in doing so, he is also explaining why Diego is in charge.

Those in charge in the other restaurants are also adaptive and flexible in their communications and responses and they, too, lead by example. Understanding guests' motives, needs and current states is pointless unless it is used to direct action. That requires emotional control and mental flexibility because, in one sense, each table in a restaurant is home to a different world. It is a place where a group of people have gathered for a specific purpose. They have their own ways of interacting, their own perspectives on standards and their own needs. They might be only a couple of metres away from the next table and yet they are locked into their own personal experience and, ultimately and reasonably, they care only about the quality of that.

For the restaurant managers and their teams, then, there is a significant level of emotional intelligence needed to be able to adapt as they move from one table to another. Each time they have only a few seconds to remind themselves which 'world' they are moving into and observe how it is currently operating.

The American psychiatrist and author M Scott Peck urged us to 'share our similarities, celebrate our differences.' An understanding of guests enables the kitchen and front of house teams to respect and respond to the differences that surround each table whilst simultaneously managing the environment, creating a sense of harmony within the room through the shared experience of sharing food. Ideally, these different worlds will coexist, each influencing the others positively, adding to the overall character and *feel* of the restaurant without ever consciously recognising the role they are playing in doing so, nor how skilfully and carefully they are being managed by the staff.

The information gathered about guests is stored for future reference. Personal preferences and requirements are logged. Knowing the people you serve means never having to be reminded. The phrase 'Welcome back' carries with it the implication of remembering and understanding. Because service is a team game the understanding has to be shared; everyone has to be welcoming and know at least as much as is necessary in order to play their part well. Information is gathered and shared before, during and after each guest's visit. Mourad Ben Tefka's comment that 'Feedback is the breakfast of champions' was perhaps an understatement. From my observations it is also lunch and dinner!

According to the Turkish proverb, 'Guests bring good luck with them.' Given the success of these restaurants that is hard to deny, particularly when guests leave so well satisfied that:

a) They are likely to return
   and

b) They are certain to share their memory positively with others.

When they do return to the restaurants, new information is updated in the light of feedback. The cycle of serving, learning and understanding continues without end.

It is a cycle that is also applied to managing and understanding staff. Julia Murrell's philosophy at Le Manoir – that 'If we are seeking to provide five-star service to our guests, we need to provide the same level of service to our staff. It is about seeing each member of staff as an individual investment' – is one that is shared across all three businesses and which underpins reward, motivation, delegation and training. Perhaps when Diego Masciaga described leadership as a lonely role requiring both discipline and commitment, he was making an oblique reference to the fact that senior managers are the only people who are not, at one time or another, regarded as guests? Whether he was or not, he certainly wasn't complaining. After all, neither he nor any of his peers ever said that it was easy...

Summary
The learning points in this chapter are:

1. Analysis leads to action
2. Being able to ask great questions and observe clearly are prerequisites for analysis
3. Curiosity often leads to creativity which, in turn, leads to change; be willing to change in the light of feedback
4. One approach to building a positive relationship with customers is to Match, Pace and Lead
5. Getting to know and understand customers is a continual process that happens before, during and after every interaction
6. The OODA Loop is a practical model for managing the immediacy of customer interactions
7. Staff are customers, too.

One other point to remember: the more staff come to know and understand their customers, the more likely they are to take pleasure in working for them; like all relationships everyone involved is influenced. As Alain Roux said:

'The reason I come out into the restaurant is to get feedback and to understand and learn about guests... Over time they become more than just customers. You share many things with them... The kitchen team take a lot more heart and pleasure when they know who they are cooking for.'

Ingredient No. 5

Understand the totality of the customers' experience and then exceed their expectations throughout

'That is a good book that is opened with expectation and closed with a profit.'

Amos Bronson Alcott

This ingredient comprises:
- The need to identify and manage the totality of the customers' experience
- The importance of understanding precisely what the business sells
- The relationship between measuring, creating and managing customer expectations
- Communication and its role in customer service.

Totality and a two-way street

This, our final ingredient, brings everything together – which is hardly surprising given that it focuses on the importance of understanding the totality of the customers' experience. This is of such importance because, in the very final analysis, it is against the totality of their experience that guests judge these three restaurants.

It is true, of course, that guests are drawn to them in the first place primarily because of the reputations of the restaurant and the chef. After all, we are living in an age when, perhaps more than ever, chefs are recognised as celebrities. The widespread interest in both their craft and them as individuals is a powerful marketing agent, one that plays a significant role in creating high expectations in the guests' minds. However, the extent to which these expectations are met and/or exceeded is determined by far more than just the quality of the food or the charisma of the chef.

Although the cuisine is undoubtedly central to the experience, it is not the only factor. Indeed, it was evident in all three restaurants that the emphasis was placed on creating a complete experience in which every element was comparable to the standard of the food. Everyone was aware that they were involved in selling much more than a meal; that a visit to each location was more akin to an event than a simple lunch or dinner. Philip Newman-Hall emphasised this point when he compared a visit to Le Manoir to other such aspirational experiences as a helicopter ride or a weekend in Paris.

In order to manage the totality of this experience, managers and every member of their team have to know precisely what it comprises. This may seem a simple and obvious point, yet it is filled with complexity. It connects the need for a clear sense of identity and vision with the role of recruitment and selection and, especially, a thorough induction programme so that staff understand every aspect of the business. It reminds us of location management and the Perimeter Principle, the importance of combining attention to detail with big-picture awareness, the value of understanding guests and why great time management is so important.

To have a chance of achieving excellence, though, managers have to do more than simply understand every possible part of the guests' experience: they have to ensure that is all connected; that it combines to create something that is so congruent and right it appears to be at once simplistic and wonderful, obvious and inspiring. The American writer Joseph Conrad could have been discussing this totality when he wrote, 'There was a completeness in it, something solid like a principle, and masterful like an instinct – a disclosure of something secret – of that hidden something.'

My study suggests that Conrad's 'hidden something' is not only revealed through the completeness; it is the completeness itself. To reach this level of congruency, managers need to set and achieve a range of process-related outcomes en route to the desired end outcome. They have to understand that this connectivity is the result of a mixture of elements all delivered and managed to the highest standard; each adds its own significant essence, adding value and joining in seamlessly to the creation of the overall experience.

In each of the three restaurants this understanding is the starting point for all day-to-day operations and all strategic planning. The senior managers and their staff know that, even though the work of the chef and his kitchen brigade is at the core of the business, what they are actually selling is the totality of the guests' experience. This begins with the very first contact on the virtual perimeter and it ends only when the location has been departed. It is influenced by every aspect of the environment, from the entrance and the car park to the corridors and the public bathrooms. It includes every facility, every product, every service, and every individual interaction between staff and guests. The aim is easy to state. It is this:

Every part of the environment with which guests might engage has to be functional and appealing and in keeping with our identity and purpose; every member of staff has to be skilled, 'on message', and determined to excel; every communication has to be an example of well-packaged honesty, sequenced appropriately. In short, every aspect of our business, every detail, is like a piece in a jigsaw; it has to play its part in building the overall picture. Everything has to fit perfectly.

This is the most demanding of requirements, not least because there are so many variables involved and, as we have already discussed, because there is a gap between excellence and perfection. It seems to me, though, having observed these people and these places for an extended period of time, that it is their willingness to pursue this goal, their determination to be masterful, that is the reason for their acknowledged high standards. It is why, sometimes, they get as close to perfection as anyone in any domain ever does.

Kingman Brewster, the American educator, wrote, 'There is no greater challenge than to have someone relying on you; no greater satisfaction than to vindicate his expectation.' It was clear to me that everyone who works in these restaurants is acutely aware that they are relied upon by their managers, their team-mates and, most importantly, their guests. Everyone understands their role, how and why others need them to get it right, and how it fits into the big picture. I came to understand that, no matter how great the expectations of their guests, the staff had even higher expectations of themselves.

Understanding is, it seems, as Eleanor Roosevelt suggested, 'a two-way street.' From my perspective it was clear that at The Waterside, Le Manoir and Gidleigh expectation management ran two ways. Everyone from the most senior managers to the newest recruit understood:

a) The totality of the experience they offered and just how well they offered it

b) That no matter how well they offered it, there is always room for improvement.

The message is: if you want to exceed the highest of customer expectations, ensure that everyone you employ has even higher ones!

The key to everything

Customer expectations are a customer's vision of a future state or action that they believe should occur because of their engagement with a provider. Expectations are more powerful than requirements and they are inevitable. There appears to be an instinct within human beings that makes us imagine and then *expect* what we think is most likely to happen in any given scenario. We base our level of expectation on a range of available information and on the sources from which that information stems. Word of mouth is a powerful influencer, although the actual nature and power of the influence it creates within us is determined by the words that are used and, more significantly, which mouth they come out of. On a more formal level, marketing media is perhaps the most obvious creator of expectations. Language and images of places and people, self-image and personal or social need, cost and location, can all help shape expectation.

Managing such expectations well is critical for business success. In the customer's mind the value of every business is determined by how well that business measures up to their expectations. And, because expectations can develop from a variety of sources and exist only in the mind of the person, there might well be an unreasonable gap between what is expected and what can actually be delivered – even if the business is brilliant. Expectations not only affect how the customer evaluates the business; they also influence all of their actions and decisions when engaging with the business. The management task, then, with regard to expectations is to:

- Set
- Monitor
- Influence
- Measure.

Set

The restaurants use a variety of methods and media to set expectations in the minds of potential customers, and these are applied across the various perimeters of the business. Given that the setting of expectations should begin at the very first point of contact between the customer and the business, the elements of the virtual perimeter play a vital role. Their websites and marketing materials are designed to highlight luxury, high quality and the sense of completeness discussed earlier. Receptionists are welcoming, professional and are expected to demonstrate their understanding of the totality of the guests' experience. Nothing is left to chance. At Le Manoir, for example, members of the reservations team are assessed against more than thirty criteria. Whatever expectations the caller has when they pick up the phone have to be matched at least and, ideally, exceeded. The standard is being set for all subsequent interactions with the guest; the rest of the team now have to live up to the promise implicit in that first conversation.

Expectations are also set through the media appearances of the key figures from each restaurant, the books they write, the articles written about them and the accolades they have earned. I have already discussed the power of the leader in the role of figurehead, expert or visionary. This power extends into the creation of customer expectations. Even if guests don't meet Raymond Blanc when they visit Le Manoir, they instinctively expect the place, the food and the service to remind them of the charismatic character they have seen on TV. And that is what happens. Whenever Michael Caines champions local produce, he knows that is creating an expectation in the minds of future visitors to Gidleigh Park, and he is comfortable doing so because his menu always matches that expectation. Guests attracted to The Waterside Inn by the stories of a culinary dynasty, expecting to be reminded of this history, walk into the reception to see the family photos adorning the walls and a selection of Michel Roux Snr's cookery books on show and for sale.

The widely accepted principle when setting expectations is to set them high enough to attract people to you and yet of a standard that you are sure you can exceed. When you have worked hard to establish a reputation for excellence, as each of the restaurants has, this becomes a much more difficult balancing act. Truthfully, I saw no indication that any of them were focusing primarily on managing the level of expectation they were creating in their customers. Rather, they focused instead on improving every aspect of their operation, with their communications on the virtual perimeter designed to begin the guests' experience well and/or to share who they are and what they do as clearly as possible. They do the latter particularly well through their engagement with TV, radio and national media.

The inescapable fact is that every time we communicate, we influence. To communicate effectively, then, we have to determine what specific influence we want to create and how best to do it. The restaurants are all excellent at creating media stories that keep them in the spotlight and serve to reinforce their unique qualities. They continually find ways to make themselves newsworthy; that highlight not just the quality of the cuisine but also the unique selling points of each business. They know that their reputations are well established and they are skilled at encouraging the media to work on their behalf.

The television programmes, interviews and articles about the business or a key individual associated with it, appear to give information or offer education and entertainment rather than advertise. Of course, they do it all. They also help to set expectations. They do so, however, without making any explicit promises to potential customers. The media simply reinforces the standing of these establishments and that is sufficient to maintain their profile and attract custom. The restaurants demonstrate how important it is continually to create stories that are newsworthy, making the press an integral part of the businesses' virtual perimeter and of their expectation management.

Irrespective of how much media coverage they create, the restaurants seem to give more attention to building the expectations of their staff than they do their customers. At least, they do so more directly. The American Engineer Charles F. Kettering said, 'High achievement always takes place in the context of high expectation.' This could be the mantra in each business. Staff are trained, encouraged and expected to perform to the best of their ability, and are then required to learn how to get better. It is such a consistent and coherent part of each culture that it has made me question whether organisations should prioritise managing staff expectations even more than they do those of customers, especially when corporate communications are aiming to set customer expectations at a high level. Perhaps the most important question a manager can ask a member of their team is:

'Do you have a higher expectation of what you – and we – can offer than our customers do?'

If the answer is a convincing *'Yes'* then commitment to ongoing improvement would seem likely. If the answer is not convincing, additional training is needed and the rigour of the recruitment process might benefit from examination. On a more global level, there certainly needs to be a positive connection between the communication shared on the virtual perimeter and the quality of the actual customer experience.

Monitor and Influence

Monitoring and understanding the level of expectations can be applied equally to staff and guests. The bottom line is that you cannot manage expectations unless you monitor them, which means that they have to be recognised before they can be addressed. This takes us back to the ability to understand those around us, to ask great questions and observe accurately.

The restaurants tend to focus on identifying the guests' reasons for visiting. One of the taken-for-granted assumptions in all three businesses is that every guest has only the highest of expectations. The importance placed on understanding guests' specific needs, as discussed in the previous chapter, plays a significant role in enabling the staff to manage these high expectations. The deliberate and subtle observation of guests plays an equally significant role; the more staff can identify guests' implicit or explicit measures of success, the more easily they can meet and even exceed them.

In the simplest of terms, guests are happy for as long as their expectations are being met; they become delighted when their expectations are exceeded. The quality of the communication between staff and guests, combined with the quality of facilities and the impact of the overall environment, influences their evaluation. During service, senior staff are especially skilled at engaging with guests, many of whom want to know about ingredients and cooking techniques. During the course of their conversations, these staff are able to highlight the quality of the dish being served and the expertise needed to produce it. It is another win-win situation, with guests being influenced positively as they learn about the secrets of the kitchen.

I am not suggesting here that the motive of staff in such situations is to manage expectations. Actually, my sense was that they were simply delighted to be able to share their enthusiasm and knowledge. It was a reflection of their desire to serve rather than anything else. However it did emphasise the importance of teaching the customer about the quality of their experience. After all, sometimes expectations and experience can blinker perception. Few guests will have the skill to realise just how much work has gone into creating a sauce or cooking a dessert. You might remember the section in The Waterside Inn story titled *Building a Salad* in which I described the detail and care that went into plating what seemed to be a few simple leaves. As a diner, I would not have paused to consider, or therefore appreciate, the qualities of the dish. It makes sense, then, to spend some time at least providing enough information to make sure that customers value the product and service they are experiencing. This would be especially true when the professionals are aiming to make everything seem as effortless as possible.

One final point is that there is obviously an ethical requirement here. Making reference to quality, originality or skill where none exists is to attempt to mislead or manipulate. This is quite clearly not what is being suggested. Highlighting examples of genuine good practice, though, in an engaging manner is a powerful and legitimate way of influencing customers.

Measure

Sam Walton said, 'High expectations are the key to everything.' The continual monitoring of expectations allows for them to be measured as well as influenced. Knowing how your customers are feeling *right now* is the prerequisite to managing their experience. Without this awareness they cannot be matched appropriately, and a strong belief in the quality of your provision can limit your capacity to measure precisely how customers are actually responding.

This is another of the many paradoxes upon which successful businesses are built: staff need to be passionate about what they do, be committed to achieving the highest standards, and believe in the value of the customer's experience. As Damien Bastiat said, 'This is not just a job, it's a lot more than that. You have to love what you are doing.' And, despite that love, staff also need to be able to recognise when, for whatever reason, customer satisfaction and expectation are diminishing. They then need to be willing to do what they can to correct it. This requires, once again, a high level of emotional control and social awareness. If, for example, Edouard Oger at Gidleigh Park is told by a guest that a bottle of wine that he has already tasted is off, he simply apologises and replaces it. Each of the restaurants has clearly defined boundaries within which they will do everything they can to accommodate guests' requests and attitudes. Guests, however, are expected to recognise and remain within these boundaries. It is a crucial part of the business-customer relationship, bringing together the expectations of the restaurant and those of their guests. All three restaurants are skilled at simultaneously demonstrating those boundaries and welcoming the many differences that guests bring. The result is a form of unspoken agreement that leads, more often than not, to the desired outcome.

This ability to define the nature of the relationship in ways that are at once subtle, positive and unmistakeable helps to reinforce both corporate identity and the unique nature of the guests' experience. It also helps staff to influence, measure and manage levels of customer expectation.

One other way expectations are managed is on the rare occasion when a genuine mistake occurs. The approach to mistake management, shared by all of the restaurants, can be summarised in the following steps:

1) Regret it
2) Use it as an immediate opportunity to exceed customer expectations
3) Learn from it.

Although staff do everything in their power to avoid making a mistake, there is an inevitability about human error. Sooner or later something will not go according to plan. When that happens the opportunity to create a new experience so positive and unexpected that it, and not the error itself, will be the focus of the guest's future story is seized with both hands. Mistakes, although to be avoided if at all possible, can become a source of guests' delight if managed well. This is a reinforcement of the point made earlier about the power of endings. The key is to follow the mistake with something that is wonderfully memorable, to provide an ending of such quality that it exceeds expectations.

Sam Walton's observation about high expectations is a reminder to professionals that if they create such expectations within their customers they have an obligation at least to match them. To do this they need the skills, resources, and the mixture of discipline and enthusiasm that leads to quality and consistency. They need to be alert and adaptive within the framework of their operation, recognising the customers' starting point, meeting and matching them there before leading them into a most delightful experience. George Bernard Shaw wrote, 'The only man who behaves sensibly is my tailor; he takes my measurements anew every time he sees me, while all the rest go on with their old measurements and **expect** me to fit them.' The restaurants measure guests anew every time they meet them. It is an inevitable consequence of their curiosity and creativity. It is part of who they are and how they manage expectations. It underpins their commitment to exceptional customer service.

Doing well along the extra mile

Of all the terms and phrases that are used to describe, explain or discuss business principles and practices, perhaps the one that is most abused is *customer service*. Somewhere on the virtual perimeter of just about every business in every industry we can find the claim to offer 'outstanding customer service' – which, by definition, cannot be true. Only a limited few can ever be outstanding at any one time. That is what the descriptor denotes. That is why there are only a few outstanding restaurants in this book.

I guess that so many businesses make the claim for great customer service because:

a) They recognise how important it is for business success
b) They are unclear about how difficult it is to achieve and maintain it.

I would argue that brilliant customer service is the result of our five ingredients mixed and managed to the highest standards. Indeed, perhaps everything I have studied and written about in this book comes together under this heading. The passion shared by so many of the people in the restaurants is, regardless of their individual areas of expertise, ultimately a passion to serve. The cause that drives them and creates their own high expectations; the systems in place, including recruitment and selection, the management of their environments and the integration of perimeters; the emphasis on exceptional teamwork; the focus on continual training and development; the use of only the very best produce; the building of relationships with suppliers and neighbours; the integration into local communities; the sense that each day is a new performance; the attention to detail and the creation and implementation of strategies; the way feedback is valued; the willingness to change, and the consistency – above all else, the consistency – of their approach, day after day, year after year, demonstrate these restaurants' commitment to service.

The American businessman and legendary quarterback Roger Staubach wrote, 'There are no traffic jams along the extra mile.' The restaurants maintain their momentum because they have all operated for many years along that extra mile. It is the only place where great customer service, indeed, brilliance of every kind, is to be found. Of course, continuous momentum is dependent upon continued energy, the source of which is passion. These are businesses in which passionate people care enough to want always to learn more and get better. They understand the totality of their guests' experience. They know that any chain is only as strong as its weakest link and that exceptional customer service is dependent upon the quality of those connections, and the relationships built between staff and guests.

Interestingly, when I studied the restaurants' websites I couldn't find any use of the term *customer service*. Instead, they all just share their identity and their vision. They show who they are and what they offer. They let their awards, their history, their reviews and their environments speak for them. They introduce key members of the team. They talk of their location. They offer an invitation.

As customers, our expectations are influenced by what we see and what we hear, by our experience and interpretation of it. We measure businesses by the relationship between their promises, implied or otherwise, and their subsequent actions and outputs. To be truly outstanding, businesses have to exceed expectations throughout every aspect of the customer experience. Benjamin Franklin wrote, 'Well done is better than well said.' The restaurants I have studied all do well.

Summary

The learning points in this chapter are:

1. The totality of the customer's experience needs to be understood by every member of staff
2. Every part of the business needs to fit perfectly
3. Customer expectations are inevitable
4. Expectations can be: set, monitored, influenced, measured
5. Staff expectations are also inevitable; aim for them to be higher than those of the customers
6. Remember that customers need to be educated about the qualities of the business, as well as served

7. Exceptional customer service is the result of excellence throughout the business; it is found along the extra mile.

One other point to remember: it is easier to identify and discuss essential ingredients for business success than it is to describe what they actually create when they are combined brilliantly. Charles Handy, the Irish author, philosopher and specialist in organisational behaviour and management, explained it thus:

'The companies that survive longest are the ones that work out what they uniquely can give to the world – not just growth or money but their excellence, their respect for others, or their ability to make people happy. Some call these things a soul.'

Success, then, for all its obvious measures, is as dependent on the intangible as it is on the tangible. It is more emotional than it is logical. It can be measured by memories as well as it can by numbers. It is determined by service even more than it is by the product. It requires passion before skill. To have any chance of being successful you have to get the ingredients right.